...im for

...ond Principle

"*The 15 Second Principle* is full of practical and powerful wisdom. With powerful illustrations that drive home his points, Al Secunda entertains as he informs. I couldn't put this fabulous book down. I highly recommend it."

—**Jack Canfield,** coauthor, *Chicken Soup for the Soul*

"Al Secunda can play a game of tennis against himself, on both sides of the court! And win every time! His lessons for life are here for all of us to know and use." —**Ray Bradbury**

"By helping people examine the beliefs and thoughts that limit them, *The 15 Second Principle* can bring its readers more productive, passionate, and creative lives. These personal stories are universal and timeless."

—**Deepak Chopra, M.D.,** Director of Educational Programs, The Chopra Center for Well-Being, La Jolla, California

"I find *The 15 Second Principle* delightful, full of insight, very human, useful and applicable in many ways. I enjoyed the stories and 'theories' and have started already to use *The 15 Second Principle.*"

—**Jacqueline Bisset**

"Al Secunda has added to his talents by turning out an unusual and arresting book. If you're like most of us who find it impossible to keep our closets neat and our desks shipshape, run, don't walk, to the nearest book shop. You'll find this book pointing the way to more freedom in your life in ways you've never dreamt of before." —**John Forsythe**

"Al Secunda is a rare combination of master student and masterful teacher. And he is committed to sharing his knowledge. Learn what he has learned."

—**Steven Carter,** author of *Getting to Commitment*

The 15 Second Principle

Short, Simple

Steps to Achieving

Long-Terms Goals

Al Secunda

Thorsons

Thorsons
An Imprint of HarperCollins*Publishers*
77–85 Fulham Palace Road,
Hammersmith, London W6 8JB

The Thorsons website address is: www.thorsons.com

First published 1999 by The Berkley Publishing Group,
a division of Penguin Putnam Inc., 375 Hudson
Street, New York, NY 10014, USA
This edition published by Thorsons 1999

1 3 5 7 9 10 8 6 4 2

© Al Secunda 1999

Al Secunda asserts the moral right to
be identified as the author of this work

A catalogue record for this book
is available from the British Library

ISBN 0 7225 3963 0

Printed and bound in Great Britain by
Caledonian International Book Manufacturing Ltd, Glasgow

In loving memory of my wonderful mother, Bernice Secunda, who gave me life and so much love. Mom, you are missed more than words can ever express.

For my friends who became my teachers, and my teachers who became my friends. The world is a more loving, wiser, and better place because of you and a sadder place because you no longer with us

Stephanie Bernstein	Peter Hammer
Lloyd Bridges	Moe Keating
Tad Danielewski	Joe Scott
Bob Gold	Zavier

While my name appears as the author of this book, many people were responsible for nurturing, helping, loving, and rejuvenating me along the way. I never would have been able to write this book without:

Cynthia Chaillie – More than any other person, Cynthia gave me the support, encouragement, guidance, and nourishment that enabled me to pursue my quest. She is my friend, coach, teacher, personal editor, and mother of this book.

Lou Secunda (my hero) – For being my loving, spectacular, dedicated, generous, youthful, balanced, and supportive father, as well as a great friend.

Judy Secunda William – For being the best sister I could ever wish for, and for all of her help, interest, love, and caring throughout my life.

Stan Corwin – for being a great agent and mentor, and for his commitment, creativity, and caring.

Hillary Cige – For believing in my journey, relating to my mission, and for recognizing the validity in this material.

Marjorie Rothstein – For her love, encouragement, friendship, creativity, courage, and for believing in me and my dream.

Vita Chen – For her friendship, vision, love, craft, faith, stamina, imagination, and master coaching.

Frederick Friedel – For his love, assistance, fearlessness, talent, and for helping me to see myself more clearly.

Dr. James Gottfurcht – For his support, editing, commitment, wisdom, perceptions, and encouragement.

Breck Costin – For his incredible distillations, unique insights, bravery, and generosity of spirit.

EXTRA SPECIAL THANKS TO: Eva Beyler, Kim Burnham, Steven Carter, James Coburn, St. John Colon, Corky Cramer, Terry, MJ, and Casey Deck, Dr. Jack Delchamps, Billy Drago, Bo Eason, Don Enright, Silvana Gallardo, The Geldon Clan, The Glaser Clan, Leona Gold, Bob and Nancy Goodman, Berry Gordy, Karen Greenhouse, Lee Case Grillo, Chris Grillo, David Hannon, Alan Hecht, Mark Helliger, Bill Jordan, Chip and Annie Kaplan, Dr. Ellie Katz, Dr. Helen Leifer, Wallace Leifer, Neil "Ernie" Levine, Jay Lubinsky, Dr. Robert Mauer, Cissy Muller, Martin Mulligan, Anubhav Oberoi, Karl Owens, Grace Paik, Suzie Pan, Leonard Post, Alberto Rizzo, Diana Ross, Larry Schonbrunn, Esq., Laurie Schumann, The Secunda Clan, The Sheingold Clan, Rodney Siegel, Michael Smollins, Stephen and Bonnie Stearns, Deborah Wakeham, Jay Wanderman, Dr. Lawrence William, Paul William, Judy and Danny Winchell, Eric Wood, and Lisa Rose William Zigmund.

ADDITIONAL THANKS TO: Paulo Alencar, The Arnold Clan, Charles Bernstein, John Boyle, Jules Bucierri, Peter Burwash, Tommy Cook, Carl Cox, Dennis Elliot, Otto Felix, Hugo Fernandez, Helene Galek, The Ganz Clan, Prof. Alan Garfinkel, Zoreh Gottfurcht, Jack and Sheba Gottlieb, Richard Greene, Steve Greene, Don Grenough, Dr. Cliff Harris, Steve "Al" Hoffman, John Holsinger, Harry Jakobs, Paul J. Jellinek, Dr. Stephen Johnson, Dr. Marv and Fran Kaplan, Donald King (the author), Adrian Lambert, Ed and Ginny Lew, Richard and Emmie Lewis, Charlotte and Sol Lobe, Laara Maxwell, Audrey Mednick, Dr. Saul Miller, Charles J. Millevoi, Joy Mosse, John Pierre, Laura Prizant, Michael and Shelley Richman, Richie and Iris Ritz, Jack Rosenberg, Mark R. Schwartz, Esq., and Inez Spaulding.

contents

preface

Most of us have precious dreams and important goals; why do many of us have difficulty realizing them? What is it that stands between us and our deepest desires? Is there a way to understand these invisible barriers so that we can live our lives more fully, and achieve more of our aspirations? In the attempt to answer these questions, and to help transform our frozen fantasies into accessible dreams and tangible goals, I created *The 15 Second Principle*.

Understanding the concept of dream realization – and using it to create more passion, pleasure, and productivity in my life – has been an extremely challenging mission. There always seemed to be one more obstacle to overcome, one more nuance to learn, and an endless stream of problems to deal with. From stammering to dyslexia, from stage fright to low self-esteem, from exhaustion to self-doubt, I had my work cut out for me. In addition, the deeper I delved into dream realization, the more I recognized limiting patterns and restraining thoughts that were defining my life and designing my future. While I knew I had talent and possibility, I realized that, left to my own devices, I was never going to tap into my full potential or achieve my precious dreams.

What I ultimately had to face was that my most treasured desires were off-limits to me. Because I didn't have the courage and discipline to visit the restricted areas of Dreamtown, I was powerless to pursue and attain the things I cherished most. In addition, I was becoming overwhelmed by the mundane chores of daily life. Whether it was making reservations on an airline, starting to gather my income tax information, or looking for a new computer, I found it a struggle to begin and finish most tasks. As a result, I became the Prince of Procrastination. What I yearned for was a self-intervention technique that would allow me to take back control of my own life.

The 15 Second Principle contains my personal journey as I attempted to learn more about the craft of dream realization, performing excellence, and the artful balance of living. Because of my eclectic career choices, my discoveries occurred in a variety of arenas: business, the performing arts, psychology, sports, metaphysics, and Eastern thought. In addition, I uncovered many pieces of the mastery puzzle by learning the philosophies and techniques of some of the most successful celebrities in Hollywood.

One of my most valuable insights was that I didn't always have to be seeking major breakthroughs in my life. Instead, I developed a deep respect and appreciation for *mini-breakthroughs.* Once I understood that an enormous amount of growth could occur by taking very small and incremental *mini-actions,* I abandoned my quick-fix, major-breakthrough approach to life. Instead, I developed a mini-action program to living. Mini-actions are brief forays into the world of our dreams, as well as quick probes into our daily tasks. These exploratory sojourns need not last long. Although mini-actions are small in scope and short in time, they are surprisingly potent in the results they can produce. They can help us face the fears and shrink the barriers that stand between ourselves and the people we can ultimately become.

A majority of this material is presented in story form. Stories have the unique ability to flow into our hearts and linger in our minds. They can also turn the reading experience into a more enjoyable and inspirational journey. Hopefully, the messages in this book will help you to become more impassioned, curious, forgiving, inventive, and disciplined as you pursue your lifelong dreams as well as perform the mundane tasks of living. By applying the principles in this book, you will experience more freedom, excitement, excellence, and self-acceptance as you travel through this challenging and unpredictable maze called life.

Keep remembering that just by adding an apostrophe and a space, you can take the word *impossible* and magically turn it into *I'm possible*. Welcome to *The 15 Second Principle*.

The 15 Second Principle

introduction

Follow your dreams or face your fears;
more often than not they will lead you to
the same wonderful destination.

— *Al Secunda*

Seeking fulfillment in our lives brings with it four basic challenges and realities. First, many of us don't seem to have enough time to do the things we want and need to do. Second, it is not easy to alter any pattern or habit in our personal and professional lives. Third, resisting or denying the technological wave that is rapidly carrying us forward is not an efficient use of our time and energy. And fourth, following our lifelong dreams and facing overwhelming tasks are quite difficult. While we may be productive and disciplined in some areas, in others we just can't seem to get going. However, becoming more efficient, disciplined, adaptive, forgiving, and courageous will be vitally important to our success and well-being.

Honing Our Success and Satisfaction Skills

The easiest way to face these four challenges and to experience more success and satisfaction is by embracing all aspects of change. This includes external change (for example, the computer and digital world) as well as internal change (such as self-awareness, self-acceptance, and self-discipline). The more we can transform our relationship with change, the more facile, creative, and curious we will become.

If we intend to keep growing and expanding our horizons, we will also need to understand the arena of freedom. This includes the freedom to act and the freedom not to act. The freedom to act means that you are able to take actions in any area of your life, such as interviewing for a new job, joining a gym, seeking out a psychologist, learning an instrument or sport, or writing a novel. The freedom *not* to act means that you are able *not* to take actions even though you have a burning desire to do so. This would include not taking addictive substances, not repeating unproductive patterns, not verbally lashing out at someone, and not seeking unhealthy relationships. Said another way, acting from a position of freedom will enable you to start doing things you know you should be doing, and to stop doing things you know you shouldn't be doing.

What Exactly Is The 15 Second Principle?

One of the components of The 15 Second Principle is an agreement. It states that you agree to give your full attention to and take some action toward a dream project, an overwhelming task, or new skill each and every day for a *minimum* of 15 seconds. In signing The 15 Second Agreement, you agree to visit the world of your dream project, challenging task or overwhelming assigment for at least 15 seconds a day. This simple yet powerful discipline will enable you to bridge the gap between rumination and creation on a daily basis. This skill will enhance your tenacity, discipline, and productivity. The principle also requires that you forgive yourself whenever you do not live up to this seemingly easy contract. (The entire agreement will be described in much more depth in the next section.)

How to Interpret 15 Seconds

The 15 seconds that we will be discussing is more a theoretical concept and less a literal definition of time. For all practical purposes, the actual time frame can be as little as one second or as much as several minutes. I am not suggesting that you use a stopwatch when applying this principle. For myself, my students, and clients, 15 seconds tends to be an unintimidating amount of psychological time. It gives you the freedom to break up patterns, change directions, and test unknown waters by allowing you to commit to new behavior for brief periods of time. Ultimately, you want to develop the ability to control whether or not you take actions on a more regular basis.

Get It Rolling

Let's say that you own an old sports car and you discover that the battery is dead. Your mission is to jump-start it. The most difficult part of this task is getting the car to begin rolling forward from its stationary position. Once you get the car moving from zero to one mile an hour, it will be much easier to increase its speed. This, in turn, helps the engine to turn over so that when you put the car into first gear the engine will start.

The same concept is true when it comes to breaking through your personal and professional inertia. Going from doing nothing to doing something is what is most important. Initially, the quality or quantity of this "something" does not really matter. It is not important how large or small, how precise or imprecise the first action is. What's most important is that you develop the ability to go from stillness to movement. What we are talking about is the ability to create momentum. Momentum is the tendency to stay in motion once you have overcome inertia. It has the unique quality of creating a self-sustaining flow and energy. The challenge is to create momentum in spite of fearful or lethargic feelings. Once you can develop the muscle of momentum, following any dream or facing any task will become an easier and less intimidating experience. With this in mind, let's keep the momentum going by beginning our journey.

1

The 15 Second Principle

This bright new day, complete with twenty-four hours of opportunities, choices, and attitudes. A perfectly matched set of 1,440 minutes. This unique gift, this one day, cannot be exchanged, replaced, or refunded. Handle with care. Make the most of it. There is only one to a customer.

—*Anonymous*

We all know that dreams are wonderful things to have, whether we dream of returning to school to complete a degree, changing careers, writing a screenplay, signing up for a class, buying a computer, learning a foreign language, or taking up a sport or musical instrument. But if we never pursue and realize any of our dreams, they can become more of a curse than a blessing. Unfulfilled dreams have the capacity to haunt us, to remind us of what we haven't done and who we haven't become. When we don't pursue these dreams, our rationale for postponing them must get stronger and more intelligent. Ultimately, we can become so articulate and logical with our reasons for not pursuing our dreams that sometimes even we will buy into our own rationalizations. Somewhere, however, deep down inside us, we know that our story is not true.

When dreams go unexplored, they can leave an enormous hole in the soul. Many of us try substitute remedies, but to no avail. From vacations to new homes, new spouses to different jobs, new cars to addictive substances, we try to seek satisfaction from indirect sources. These diversionary tactics may offer temporary relief, but ultimately, they will become a major distraction in our quest for self-fulfillment. The biggest dilemma here is that nothing can fill the void except stepping onto and traveling down the dream path. Fortunately or unfortunately, there is no substitute for the satisfaction we receive when we walk directly toward and engage our personal dreams. It's always fascinating to listen to senior citizens talk about their lives. What they usually regret the most is not that they didn't succeed at everything they tried, but rather that they didn't risk, dare, and stretch in the direction of their passions. As an elderly woman once said to me, "Who was I so afraid of becoming – myself?"

If the price we pay for neglecting our dreams is so huge, then why aren't we dedicating more time and energy to realizing them? I believe there are two reasons for this. First, it is very difficult psychologically to cross the line and enter the world of our most precious dream or dreams. Somehow we feel it's safer to keep our dreams protected in the world of untouched, idealized, and idolized fantasies. Second, even if we muster our courage and cross this tender threshold, it is very difficult to remain in the self-gifting realm of Dreamland. Fear of failing, fear of succeeding, fear of becoming ourselves, and fear of turning a holographic fantasy into a tangible reality can all be powerful deterrents. Is it any wonder then that most of us will spend more effort designing elaborate schemes to avoid confronting these emotions and situations than we will spend finding ways to face them? Apparently we believe it is much easier to avoid perceived pain than it is to pursue mastery and fortify our character.

After exploring the dream fulfillment issue for many years, I created a process that has helped me, my students, and my clients to cross the thresholds of our dreams on a more regular basis. It's called The 15 Second Principle. It is based on one simple premise: *Either we don't really care about our dreams, or we are scared to death of them.* Our brain will try to find loopholes, exceptions, and footnotes to this very direct statement, but most of the time, this sentence will ring true. Emotionally speaking, a dream is either too cold (we don't really care about it) or it's too hot (we care a lot about it). The 15 Second Principle is designed to help us discover which one it is. The principle has two parts – and each one is equally important as the other.

Part One: Spend a Minimum of 15 Seconds a Day Furthering the Project

In this hectic world, we can conveniently rationalize that we were too busy on a given day to devote an hour, thirty minutes, or even fifteen minutes to a dream project. While this may or may not be true, what happens on any busy day is that we wind up doing nothing on it. Then the next day comes and once again we are just too busy to devote these precious blocks of time to our project. After a week, month, or year of this behavior, two things are usually true: First, nothing much has gotten accomplished. Second, inertia has set in. Habits breed habits. From not going to the gym to not practicing a sport or musical instrument, these nonactions can become as deeply ingrained in our system as the habit of doing them can be.

Committing to The 15 Second Principle each day, however, can prevent physical and emotional inertia from setting in. It is effective in many ways:

1. Psychologically, 15 seconds is a tiny amount of time. Even if the experience turns out to be sheer hell, you can put up with the pain for at least 15 seconds. If it's that uncomfortable an experience, your agreement states that you can stop this self-inflicted torture. This escape clause makes it easier for you to keep returning to your project for a *minimum* of 15 seconds each day.
2. It will encourage you to take charge of the project and to experience it every day (even if it's for only 15 seconds). This will prevent your fears and negative thoughts from growing too large. By momentarily taking the helm of your dream ship, you will have a visceral experience of what living your dream is really about.
3. You can never convince yourself or anyone else that you don't have 15 seconds on a given day to do something. It's too small a block of time to rationalize away. As a result, you have to face the truth. Either you don't *really* care about this thing, or you are scared to death of it. Suddenly there are no gray ambivalent areas within which to hide. For at least 15 seconds a day you must squarely face yourself.

4. Although you are only committing to 15 seconds, you will generally find that you will want to do more. It's the fear of beginning rather than the actual doing of the project that is preventing you from spending more time pursuing your dreams. The first 15 seconds of practicing or doing anything is psychologically the hardest. If 15 seconds pass and you are still having a miserable time, give yourself permission to stop. You have lived up to your agreement. If, on the other hand, you are energized or have a little discipline, just do a little more.
5. The earlier in the day that you can log in your 15 seconds, the easier it will become to return to this project during the day.
6. The 15 Second Principle will also allow you to stop and detach yourself from your usual mind-set and behavior. This momentary intervention will help you to separate yourself from obsolete patterns and enable you to gain a clearer perspective and deeper awareness of your life and restricting habits.

Part Two: Forgive Yourself When You Don't Do Your 15 Seconds Each Day

On the surface, The 15 Second Principle appears to be simple and easy. You probably have no doubt that you can fulfill your daily time obligation every day. "No problem. Any fool can commit to something for 15 seconds a day," you will say. Think again. You will be shocked at how challenging this exercise is. This is especially true if you pick a cherished dream project. The main point here is that if you screw up and skip a day, *forgive yourself.* Berating yourself will just make it more difficult for you to get back on track the following day.

THE 15 SECOND DREAM AGREEMENT FOR:

_____

(Please enter title of dream project)

On this day of _____ , I agree to enter into a 15 Second Agreement for the above dream project. In addition, I understand the following:

1. Each day I will take some action that will further my dream project along. It must be a positive action and last a *minimum* of 15 seconds. (Alternatively, I agree to a Monday-through-Friday, five-day-a-week 15 Second Agreement.)

2. If I do not live up to my daily commitment, I promise to forgive myself and recommit to the rules of my dream agreement on the very next day.

3. I will continue to follow the laws of this agreement and will do so until my dream project has been completed or until I decide to renegotiate this agreement with myself.

_____

(Dream maker's signature)

Assuming you want to play this dream creation game, I have drawn up an agreement for you (above). If you are interested in signing up, it's very simple. You'll be in for a very accelerated, masterful, and enlivening journey.

For those tender souls who have a precious dream but who are unwilling or afraid to sign the agreement, there is an alternate agreement available. You simply commit to writing down your dream on a piece of paper or computer screen each day and looking at it for a minimum of 15 seconds. The only action you are committing to is writing down the dream and reading it, nothing more. Afterwards you can rip up the paper or delete it from the computer.

Once again, if and when you forget to write your dream down, you agree to forgive yourself and to recommit to your agreement on the very next day. It is totally acceptable for this process to go on for months or years. The daily action of writing down your dream and looking at it will slowly but surely give it more authenticity. This will help you to build up your courage muscle, which, in turn, will enable you ultimately to sign The 15 Second Dream Agreement.

◆ACTIONS VS. ACTIVITIES◆

> *If you don't change the direction you're going, you're likely to end up where you're headed.*
>
>   —*Chinese proverb*

Anyone pursuing excellence and well-being must learn to differentiate between two important words: *actions* and *activities*. While both connote movement and may appear to be similar, more often than not they are diametrically opposed to each other. Actions set us free, while activities have the ability to enslave us. Actions help us regain control of our lives, while activities perpetuate procrastination. Actions assist us in achieving our full potential, while activities lure us down unfulfilling and addictive paths. Actions, therefore, are endeavors that are related to fulfilling our needs, goals, and contentment.*

To help you understand the differences between these two words, imagine that a rat is placed in a cage that contains a treadmill and lots of toys. In the middle of the cage is a red lever that when pressed will open the door and set him free. If the goal of the rat is freedom, no matter how fast he runs on the treadmill or how involved he becomes with his toys, he will never gain freedom. There is only one way out of jail for this rat: going directly to the red lever and pressing it. In this example, pressing the lever is the freeing *action,* while busying himself with the treadmill and toys is the imprisoning and distracting *activity.*

The human condition is very similar to the rat's situation. Quite often, we will seek out activities that are not essential in helping us to reach our destinations. Let's look at two examples:

- If April arrives and you have not touched your tax returns, calling your accountant and setting up an emergency meeting is an *action,* while cleaning out a closet and washing your car are *activities.*

- If you desperately want to begin a dream project (writing a novel, getting an article published, doing a home aerobics program, making an oil painting), taking a step toward that project is an *action,* while going to the movies is an *activity.*

Unfortunately, when we human beings are left to our own devices, we are much more likely to direct our attention toward seductive activities rather than toward challenging actions. This is because activities are safer to approach and engage in. They tend to contain less emotional and psychological charge, which makes them less confronting. Because activities do not address our dreams, personal identities, or mastery, they tend to be easier to think about, begin, and complete. Actions, on the other hand, deal with more important core issues and can be more frightening.

In addition, activities are about staying busy or kicking back rather than about facing our full potential, fears, and responsibilities. They are more about avoidance and unfulfilling

---

* Be aware there are usually two ways to execute any action. One way can nurture us and the other can exhaust us. For example, when writing a report, we can treat the experience as either a tense and fearful one or a relaxed and energizing one. Whenever possible, create nurturing actions. See "The 15 Second Pleasure Priority" on page 60.

patterns, and less about risk, fulfillment, and the unknown. As a result, the feelings and emotional rewards we reap from completing activities are limiting. With low stakes come low payoffs. Perhaps Mick Jagger was thinking about activities when he sang, "I can't get no satisfaction." What's vital to understand is that a thousand activities cannot give you the relief and self-satisfaction of one powerful action. The following double-negative saying holds a lot of wisdom: "You can never get enough of what you don't really want."

One way to distinguish between an action and an activity is to observe how you feel *afterward*. When you feel energized and empowered after completing a task, chances are it was an action. Here are some examples:

- If you finally go back to the gym after stopping for two months, and you feel like you have taken back control of your life, it was an action.
- If you take a full day to clean out your entire garage and you feel free and in control of your life, it was an action.

On the other hand:

- If you call a friend to discuss last night's party rather than phoning a potential new customer, and afterward you feel like you squandered fifteen minutes of your life, it was an activity.
- If you watch a movie on television rather than paying bills and starting an overdue report, and you feel overwhelmed the next morning, watching television was an activity.

It's important to note that the same task might be an action one day and an activity the next. A bachelor who finally vacuums his carpet after six months is performing an action. If he continues to vacuum every day for the next month, this behavior has become a compulsive activity. A young workaholic who finally takes a vacation is performing an action. If this same executive quits her job and vacations for the next five years, she could be living out one huge activity.

By the same token, the same task can be an action for one person and an activity for another. If a relentless "party animal" shows up at one more party, this is an activity. If a shy recluse shows up at the same party, this is an action.

Bear in mind there is nothing wrong with pursuing activities as long as they are done with awareness and in moderation. We all need vacations, breaks, and escapes. What's dangerous is when we engage in a constant diet of activities and think they are actions. The skill is in differentiating between them. At any given moment, you should be able to answer the question, "What am I involved with right now, an action or an activity?" This heightened awareness can help you to select a healthier balance between them. If you can't discern the difference, how are you going to know when you are on or off track?

If performing actions make us feel so much better, why don't we do more of them? To answer this question, let's go back to the rat in the cage. Imagine that the red freeing lever is wired with electricity and that if he touches it, the rat will receive a little shock. In order to become free, he must be willing to experience some initial discomfort. Is the rat willing to deal with the electricity to gain his freedom? Is he willing to experience a little pain for a lot of adventure and satisfaction?

It is also interesting to think about how the rat will react to his own freedom if he sets himself free. Will he thrive with all of his new space and freedom, or will he become overwhelmed with the expansiveness of his new world? Will he enjoy taking responsibility for his life, or will he miss blaming his cage for everything he hasn't accomplished? Will he flourish in challenging and unfamiliar settings, or will he retreat back to the confines of his safe, familiar, and limited cage? Once free, will the rat feel so uncomfortable with all the spaciousness, and overwhelmed with the responsibility of liberty, that he will do what Erich Fromm refers to as "escape from freedom" and return to his cage?

Like the rat, in order to realize our dreams and goals we must overcome any trepidation we feel about touching our own personal red levers. While many people talk about change and satisfaction, few are willing consistently to take hold of that red lever in order to create and receive freedom and fulfillment.

Apparently, the world contains millions of bright, educated, and creative people who are afraid to grab onto their dream lever and experience a real or imagined shock.

There is some good news about our personal red levers. While we may fear that a bolt of life-threatening lightning will come out of the lever when we touch it, this is rarely the case. We may experience some initial discomfort, but it is rarely life-threatening. Rather than circling around our red levers indefinitely, the fastest way to turn inertia and frustration into motion and creativity is by listening to that quiet voice of freedom that is whispering inside our heads. This can be accomplished by courageously walking over to our personal red lever, taking a deep breath, and taking hold of it. (See "The Door Process" on page 143).

In a television interview, Barbra Streisand revealed that one of her greatest artistic insights occurred when she finally gave up the notion that performing (including directing) was supposed to be a comfortable experience. This insight occurred while she was listening to a gentleman on television. He was explaining that when we are challenging ourselves, stretching, and doing frightening things, we should not expect our initial response to be a regular and comfortable state. Barbra Streisand said:

> *It was like a revelation. Here I was thinking that this is going to be pleasant and comfortable. I'm lucky to have the privilege to be directing this movie and it doesn't say I have to be comfortable. It just cleared my mind.*

Perhaps we set up unrealistic demands when we think that performing new actions in new environments will be a comfortable process. If we expect to feel normal – to have regular physical sensations – before, during, and after grabbing onto our personal red levers, we are usually going to be disappointed. We must remember that when we take on new and challenging actions, we will experience different sensations, reactions, and emotions. Any additional adrenaline in our system, tightness in the stomach, or nausea we may feel shouldn't necessarily mean that we should stop pursuing our dreams. In fact, what these sensations might indicate is that our dream, although threatening to parts of our protective defense mechanism, is very important.

In closing, keep reminding yourself that whenever you stretch yourself by visiting new domains, feelings of your own inadequacy will usually surface. If you are waiting to feel fully competent before attempting something new and dynamic, you are not being fair to yourself or the growth process. Remember not to overdo it; stretching too much at one time can be detrimental to your health and passion. After all, there are more nurturing ways to learn how to swim than throwing yourself into the Atlantic Ocean in the middle of the winter. Instead, call upon The 15 Second Principle to help you take the next step forward.

◆THE 15 SECOND MOMENTUM LIST◆

> *Facing it—always facing it—that's the way to get through. Face it! That's enough for any man.*
> *—Joseph Conrad*

While Joseph Conrad gives us powerful advice regarding success and excellence, many of us have a difficult time facing challenging tasks and assignments on a regular basis. Rather, we tend to work in fits and starts. Either we are in procrastination and postpone what we know we have to do, or we are in overdrive, and try to make up for the time we lost procrastinating. Both habits take their mental and physical toll.

By producing more actions and less activities we will experience more freedom and momentum, which will enable us to gain more control over our personal and professional lives. However, creating momentum is a very elusive craft. To help generate more of it, it is helpful to make a momentum action list. This list is a simple yet powerful way to turn lethargy and hopelessness into excitement and possibility.

First, make a list of what you want to do tomorrow by entering each task on the left side of the page.

Then, to gain momentum on things you want to do tomorrow, do fifteen seconds of work on each one of them *today*.

Enter the work (regardless of how minimal it might appear) on the right side of the page.

THINGS TO DO TOMORROW	THINGS I ALREADY DID TODAY
Write letter to Mr. Wally	Dear Mr. Wally, Per our conversation, I am enclosing the material that you requested
Write thank-you note to Sylvia	Dear Sylvia Just a short note to say hello.
Call Joe about guitar lessons	218-287-8821
Call Sunset Restaurant	209-554-7846, Sat. 7 p.m., four people
Make shopping list and go shopping	bananas, soup, lettuce, melon
Pick up material from Robert	198 N. Weatherly St.

By spending just a few minutes today with tomorrow's list, you will be able to gain momentum with many projects. When you wake up tomorrow morning, you will already have the wind at your back as you revisit these assignments.

If you prefer, you can create this list each morning for yourself. Simply spend 15 seconds on twenty projects or tasks. The earlier in the day you begin your momentum list, the less ominous each assignment will feel later when you return to it.

Make at least seven copies of the blank momentum list and experiment with it. You have nothing to lose but the feelings of being overwhelmed and the pain derived from procrastination.

THE 15 SECOND MOMENTUM LIST

Things to Do Tomorrow	Things I Already Did Today

2

Breaking through Your Resistance

For each of us there is a deeply personal dream waiting to be discovered and fulfilled. When we cherish our dream and then invest love, creative energy, perseverance, and passion in ourselves, we will achieve an authentic success. Let your imagination soar, for it is your soul's blueprint for success.

—Sarah Ban Breathnach, *author of* Simple Abundance

I s your desire to change stronger than your actual ability to do so? If so, you are not alone. Most of us seek more advancement and positive transitions in our personal and professional lives, but very few of us seem to experience enough of them in our lifetime. If you have any doubt about this, just look at our New Year's resolutions at the beginning and again at the end of each year.

As we have been discussing, to achieve change in our lives requires taking focused actions on a more regular basis. These actions will ultimately lead to additional mini-breakthroughs. Mini-breakthroughs can be either physical, mental, or emotional. They are insights or experiences that give us greater clarity, skills, faith, confidence, and momentum.

Unfortunately, the human condition is not geared to creating mini-breakthroughs on a regular basis. Instead, we tend to have a lot of resistance when it comes to changing patterns and routines.

Either we have difficulty creating goal-oriented mini-actions or we can't sustain them. The following two personal experiences inspired me to create this chapter.

Story #1

I have always wanted to become a more organized person. This is because whenever I do get organized I always feel freer and more in control of my life. However, staying organized has not been an easy task. If you believe in transmigration of the soul, in a previous life I was probably an out-of-control monkey. Because I have spent many years improving upon my organizational skills, and embracing my monkey child within, I am able to give the illusion that this ability comes easily to me. However, if I do not remain aware and lovingly vigilant, I am capable of slipping right back into all of my old behavior. Here is an example of what I'm talking about.

One evening while preparing for bed, I took off a pair of slacks and proceeded to carry them right past the closet where they belonged. Then, in an unconscious manner, I threw them onto a chair several feet away. A split second later, I snapped out of my stupor and became a witness to my own monkey business. If I was so interested in keeping my home neat and feeling great about my environment, why in the world would I regress by carrying my pants past the appropriate closet, and then tossing them haphazardly onto a chair?

Story #2

Because I had dyslexia as a child, reading was always a tedious chore rather than a passionate endeavor. What occurred when I read was that certain words and letters would miraculously change places before my very eyes. The faster my eyes traveled, the more chaos would appear on the page. To keep all the letters and words in place, I developed slow, tense, and serious eyes. As a result, whenever I read my eyes never experienced any relaxation, flow, or physical enjoyment. Looking back at my education, I am amazed that I was able to get through graduate school with this grueling reading technique.

Through the years, I would periodically take reading courses that I hoped would make the reading experience more enjoyable. Unfortunately, nothing helped. Then, a few years ago, I signed up for a speed-reading course specifically designed for people with a history of dyslexia. A gentleman named Robert Kirby taught the class. His program coupled a group of physical actions (movement of the eyes, arms, and legs) with reading exercises. The wonderful thing about his simple approach was that my eyes began experiencing more flow, relaxation, and enjoyment. In addition, my comprehension didn't plummet. I even started to taste the soothing sensations that natural-born readers must experience.

As I began tasting my true reading potential, something interesting started to happen. On a given day I would totally forget to practice the simple four-minute workout. As soon as I became aware of my behavior, I would reenroll myself into this helpful routine. However, no sooner would I do this than I would once again forget to practice. "This is fascinating," I said to myself. "While I claim to want to improve my reading skills, whenever I begin to experience meaningful advancement, I find a way to thwart my progress. What's going on?"

The above two stories are perfect examples of one of the great human dilemmas. While most of us yearn for greater skills and self-improvement, something inside of us becomes very threatened by change. Change appears to be a pull-push experience. We pull it toward us, but once it crosses a certain intimacy threshold, something in us becomes anxious, and we push it away.

In this chapter we will explore many different facets of this self-sabotaging phenomenon. This material was especially created for people who look around and say, "With so much potential, how in the world did I wind up here?" "If I felt so much healthier and more attractive, with all of that weight off, how could I have gained it all back?" Or, "Just as I was feeling great about paying off my credit cards, why did I start charging those nonessential items again?"

After exploring the area of change, you will be better able to understand and deal with your own behavior, inertia, and self-imposed restrictions. This awareness will enable you to make adjustments and take corrective actions that will help you to become more daring, creative, and successful.

HOMEOSTASIS: TAMING THE PROTECTIVE GIANT

I'd like to offer a possible explanation for our resistance to change: homeostasis. It's actually quite simple, and it deals with human nature. Once we understand this basic concept of being human, we will be better equipped to produce more growth and aliveness. Webster defines *homeostasis* as "a relatively stable state of equilibrium or a tendency toward such a state." Two examples of homeostasis are our body's capacity to keep its temperature at a relatively constant 98.6 degrees, and our ability to remain physically balanced as we move, walk, dance, and run. These and other automatic compensating systems help to keep us alive and functioning. I believe there is also a *survival homeostasis mechanism* built into each of us. Its purpose is to maintain the status quo and to protect us just the way we are. It does not understand terms such as good or bad, healthy or unhealthy, productive or unproductive. Likewise, it doesn't care whether we are happy or sad, excited or depressed, overweight or underweight, content or angry, employed or unemployed, drug-free or drug-addicted, wealthy or poor. Rather than passing judgment about our condition, the mechanism's sole mission is to defend and perpetuate itself. The system views anything familiar as safe, and anything unfamiliar as unsafe. In a sense, it is a status quo device that pledges its allegiance to our present condition and views our current status as safe and normal.

Because of its protective nature, this homeostasis self-preservation system will be triggered whenever change is introduced into our lives. To counterbalance this change, our survival mechanism will instinctively attempt to protect the old by reinstating the more familiar state. This survival mechanism can explain why change in drastic dosages does not work permanently for many people. Let's remember Newton's Second Law of Physics: "For every action there is an equal but opposite reaction." By throwing the pendulum of change wide in one direction, we usually give it the momentum to swing back in the opposite direction with a powerful force and determination. Once we understand this natural law, we can prepare for this countercorrection, should it ever appear. With this added awareness, we can approach the entire area of progression and regression from a much more knowledgeable point of view.

Homeostasis will usually view any change as a loss. When change occurs, the mechanism will convince you that something is being taken away from you. The system does not view change from a gain or growth perspective. Rather, it is devoted to the status quo. Don't make any waves and homeostasis is ecstatic. This is why, when you make major waves – moving, changing jobs, getting married, or breaking up – homeostasis gets very activated, causing you to experience feelings of loss and withdrawal.

Looking at our resistance to change through the eyes of our homeostasis survival mechanism can help us to understand why millions of people stop dieting, exercising, practicing, and getting promoted at work. It also explains why people return to unhealthy habits and relationships. Apparently, we are more comfortable holding onto familiar problems, fears, and pains than choosing and facing new opportunities and possibilities. Once we gain awareness of this natural aversion to new environments and situations, it will become easier to understand our self-defeating behavior. It should be a relief to know that our setbacks and detours are simply the work of our automatic and protective homeostasis system and not some devious monster living within us.

Some good news about this powerful system, which is important to understand in order to have it work for you, is that while the homeostasis mechanism automatically resists sudden and excessive changes, it is less likely to get activated when slow and incremental changes are introduced. Consider the following two examples of how to view this protective homeostasis system.

I like to imagine there is a protective yet sleepy giant quietly resting inside me. I call him Homeostasis. His job is to keep me just the way I am – at any cost. If any of my behavior changes significantly, Homeostasis will feel all the movement and awake. His reaction will be to protect me by fighting or resisting the change. If, however, my behavior does not exceed a certain margin of change, and it occurs in small enough increments, Homeostasis will not feel that I am being threatened. Instead, he will view these new mini-actions as harmless or neutral, and allow them to enter. Once this adoption occurs, he will embrace and protect these new incremental changes as though they were part of the older and more familiar condition.

Next let's picture Mrs. Jones as she drives up to her home in a beautiful new black Jaguar and parks it in her driveway. After locking the car, she turns on her extra-sensitive alarm system. That night, a gentle but persistent snowstorm arrives. Late the next day, Mrs. Jones ventures out to discover her car buried in four feet of heavy snow. Why didn't the car alarm ever go off? The obvious answer is that each snowflake was so small, light, and harmless that whenever one landed on the car, the sensors in the system were not activated. The alarm was not sensitized enough or programmed to react to a snowflake as a threat. Because each snowflake was not heavy enough to trigger the alarm, the system accepted each and every one.

The first and most important principle of change is that in order to get somewhere else, we must first embrace and "own" where we currently are. Rather than fighting fat, going to war against smoking, or attacking a lateness problem, we must first develop less of an antagonistic relationship with the habit or situation we want to change. This will be discussed in greater detail in "The Inclusion Factor" on page 29.

The second principle of change is that it is usually better to introduce change in small and gradual dosages. When dieting, for example, we should think in terms of losing ounces per week and not pounds. We also should measure our progress in months and years rather than days and weeks. When exercising or practicing an instrument, we want to add minutes and not hours to our regimen. The trick is to sneak up slowly but surely on our short- and long-range goals. This will prevent the protective alarm system from getting activated and awakening a slew of concerned and frightened internal vigilantes. This is the main reason that cram courses and intense training approaches usually produce only temporary results.

In addition, whenever beginning something new or returning to an old project, we should never try to make up for lost time. In the long run, this is the worst thing we can do. This tactic will mentally and/or physically come back to haunt us in the form of injuries, exhaustion, or hopelessness. Rather, we need to trust that the human body is so talented and resilient that it has the capacity to make enormous progress as long as we stay committed to a nurturing and consistent routine. The name of the game here is slow and incremental.

For those daring warriors out there who love drastic change, major challenges, declaring war, and going cold turkey, keep remembering Newton's Second Law of Physics. You brave souls need to be alert just in case your survival mechanism sends the powerful and protective pendulum swinging back in the other direction. If this occurs, it will usually carry with it massive strength, weight, and determination as it revisits the old and more familiar habits and terrain. The more aware you are of this possibility, the better equipped you will be to deal with it.

Each story, anecdote, and exercise in *The 15 Second Principle* respects the existence and power of our homeostasis survival mechanism. A common theme that runs throughout the book is that growth need not be a drastic and suffering experience. Instead, expansion can be nurturing, nonthreatening, and slow. The book values mini-actions and views them as a powerful part of growth and momentum. Use The 15 Second Principle daily and you will discover how many more possibilities suddenly and painlessly open up to you. You will also experience that change and growth can be more of a celebratory evolution and less of a primal and forceful revolution.

BARNEY THE CAT

Let's say you've decided to share your home and heart with a cat. To fulfill this desire, you go to a local pet shelter and fall in love with a huge creature named Barney. Barney weighs in at twenty-three pounds and possesses a purr that resembles thunder. After living with Barney for a while, you discover that he has a few very interesting idiosyncrasies:

1. He will never eat or drink anything on the floor. You have to put his dishes on a high table.

2. He jumps into the bathtub whenever he senses danger.

3. He runs into the house any time he sees a bird.

4. He hates to be held.

Intrigued by these personality traits, you call the shelter to find out whether they have a record of Barney's history. Much to your delight, his previous owner had left a biography on your new roommate. You learn that Barney used to live in a household with two huge Dobermans who loved to terrorize him. If they got to his food or drink first, it would be gone. As a result, Barney's owner always had to place his food on a high table.

The two Dobermans would get their flea baths in the bathtub. Hating this experience with a vengeance, they'd never go near the bathroom unless dragged. Therefore, Barney could always find refuge by jumping into the empty bathtub whenever they chased him.

When Barney was a kitten, he discovered a baby robin that had fallen out of its nest. The mother robin, to protect her offspring, started a relentless nosediving attack on Barney. After being hit several times by the mother's sharp beak, Barney ran into the house. From that day forward, Barney was afraid of birds.

Once when Barney was being held, Rough-House, the bigger Doberman, grabbed him by the tail, pulled him out of his owner's arms, and dragged him around the house for a while. After that experience, Barney would never let anyone hold him.

All of Barney's idiosyncrasies now make total sense. *His unusual behavior was learned in direct response to his environment.* The problem is that while all of his fears were once necessary for his survival, these behaviors are no longer appropriate for his new and safer environment. He has a new owner, lives in a safer house, and the Dobermans are now chasing mailmen in downtown Detroit. Unfortunately, even though Barney no longer needs his old defense mechanisms to survive, he still perceives danger everywhere. Unless you are able to replace his fearful associations with pleasurable ones, for example by rewarding him with a cat treat each time you hold him, Barney will retain these fear-induced responses for the rest of his life.

You might think of Barney's current behavior as foolish and illogical until you remember how we as human beings also hang on to our early fears, traumas, and outdated survival mechanisms. A small child who is scared by a large dog often spends the rest of his life being afraid of dogs. A young boy who gets lost in the woods for twenty-four hours might hate the concept of camping for the rest of his life. A young girl who falls off of a step-ladder might spend the rest of her life having a fear of heights. A small boy who accidentally gets hit in the face with a ball might spend the rest of his life tensing and bracing every time a ball is thrown to him.

The tragedy here is that bringing our past fears into the present will produce more of the same outcomes. We will always be responding to certain circumstances from a prejudiced and preconceived point of perception. We will be reacting and not creatively acting. By dragging our past into the present, we will be tainting the present, which, in turn, will be limiting our future. Our challenge is to free ourselves from the effects of past traumas so that we can respond appropriately to current situations and events.

One way to free yourself from past traumatic circumstances or to lessen their impact on you is to make a list of your most painful childhood experiences. Next, write down the decisions you made about life because of these negative experiences. As an example, let's say that as a child you almost drowned in a lake. This primal experience could produce the decision that swimming is dangerous and unpleasant.

Or let's say that when you were a young boy you fell in love with the little girl next door. When you became brave enough to share your feelings with her, she seemed insulted as she laughed and ran to tell her girlfriends. Your heart was broken. You might have made the decision that being vulnerable and sharing your true feelings is not a safe or enjoyable thing to do.

The obvious question that needs to be asked is, Are these decisions still serving you? Every now and then apply The 15 Second Principle by stopping and assessing whether your early decisions and survival mechanisms are still valid and helpful today. Old fears and jaded perceptions could be placing obsolete roadblocks in front of important entryways. These barricades may be determining the roads never traveled, adventures never tasted, and people never met. In addition, the price that you pay for these off-limit constraints could include spontaneity, trust, freedom, and self-expression. This is too big a cost for any person.

◆THE INCLUSION FACTOR◆

Each of us probably has at least one quality, trait, or habit that we would like to work on and improve. Perhaps we'd prefer to be thinner, in better condition, less addicted, richer, more organized, more informed, or happier. Most of us know what we want to improve upon, but very few of us seem to be successful in achieving lasting changes in these areas.

One of the most powerful realities of change is the tenacity of what we resist. The more we attempt to rid ourselves of a habit, the more of a hold it tends to have on us. The more we try to bury a negative thought with positive thinking, the louder the negative thought can become. The more we attempt to annihilate an unwanted characteristic with vivid visualizations, the more persistent it may be. The more we try to suppress sadness with an imposed state of false happiness, the less authentic and integrated we feel. In a sense, when unwanted habits and feelings sense their survival is being threatened, they will respond by digging in their heels and fighting even harder.

This might appear to be a Catch-22 situation, but there is a way out. I offer it to you in the hope it will help to free you from the effects of limiting thoughts and habits. I call this concept *the inclusion factor.* It is a little tricky, because it is based on a paradox that will most likely challenge your belief system. The inclusion factor states that it is possible to hold two contradictory statements, feelings, or beliefs simultaneously. This is usually quite difficult to accept because we have been brought up in a culture that encourages an either/or mentality. We have not been trained to allow for two diametrically opposed emotions or ideas to live side by side. However, if we don't make room for opposite feelings, thoughts, and traits to live (or visit) under the same roof and we instead focus on eradicating the undesirable ones, the negative ones will tend to become even larger and more debilitating.

> *A fundamental neuropsychological principle is that whatever stimulus you focus on becomes magnified in your perceptual field . . . while all the other stimuli are reduced. The phenomenon is called* lateral inhibition.
>
> —*Dr. Saul Miller*
> Performing Under Pressure

The inclusion factor states that within me there is both a thin and a heavy person, a quick and a slow learner, a winner and a loser, a talented and an untalented student, an attractive and a homely person, an able and a disabled athlete, a dark and a light side, a confident and a scared person. I am a walking conglomeration of all these possibilities. Because it is an inclusive and not an either/or situation, the question can then become, Where do I want to put my attention? Do I choose to focus on nurturing my positive qualities, or do I place my attention on attacking, destroying, or worrying about my less desirable qualities?

One of the most powerful sentences you will read in this book is this: *We tend to become or be controlled by the very thing we don't want to include.* A heavy person who hates being overweight and is always attacking the extra pounds can have a weight problem for his entire life. A woman who is driven by the fear of becoming a homeless bag lady can spend the rest of her life being hounded by this feeling, regardless of how wealthy and successful she becomes. A young boy who was once hurt and ashamed when his older brother called him stupid could spend the rest of his life accumulating Ph.D.'s just to prove his brother wrong. A man who hates being disorganized and who constantly attempts to annihilate this trait can be fighting this problem forever.

The word include is a little tricky, so let's discuss it for a minute. Imagine that you own a special series of videotapes. Each tape shows you with a different characteristic in a different setting. In one video you are failing miserably, while its companion video shows you winning. In another video you are living outside as a homeless person, while its companion video shows you living in a beautiful home. One video shows you overweight, lethargic, and wearing unattractive clothing, while its companion video presents you thinner, energized, and wearing attractive garments. Another video shows you crying and moaning, "I can't, IT'S TOO LATE, this is just too difficult," while its companion video reveals you smiling and saying, "I can. I think I can figure this thing out." Still another video shows you as an angry victim saying, "No, I don't feel like doing it now," while its companion video reveals you as a determined fighter saying, "Even though I don't feel like it, I am going to honor my commitment to myself and do it anyway."

What makes these tapes so unusual is that you cannot destroy them or give them away. You are stuck with all of them forever. While I know this is not the greatest news in the world, it is not the worst news either. Because you own and house this huge video library, you always get to pick and choose which tapes you are going to see up on your large television screen. As the program manager, you have a choice as to whether your *Insecure Loser* video gathers dust on the shelf or whether it is up on the screen playing in Dolby sound day and night.

Once you make room for dualities to float side by side, you will become larger than any one of them. You will become the vessel that holds all of your characteristics (the good, the bad, and the ugly). Instead of trying to annihilate the heavy person inside of you, you will be freer to focus on building the thin and healthy person. Rather than attempting to destroy the disorganized person, you can choose to let the organized person (regardless of how feeble) take more mini-actions.

The inclusion factor will encourage you to redirect your attention and point of view. Any time you find yourself attacking a bad habit, or attempting to demolish a negative thought, stop and apply The 15 Second Principle. By stepping back from the conflict you will be able to see things more clearly. This disengagement will remind you to include more and expel less. Once you can allow intolerable thoughts and characteristics to exist within you the result will be more peace and quiet inside your mind. This, in turn, will add freedom, creativity, and focus and reduce pain, struggle, and tension.

> *I dreamed I had a child, and even in the dream I saw it*
> *was my life, and it was an idiot, and I ran away. But it*
> *always crept onto my lap again, clutched at my clothes.*
> *Until I thought, if I could kiss it, whatever in it was my*
> *own, perhaps I could sleep. And I bent to its broken face,*
> *and it was horrible. . .but I kissed it. I think one must*
> *finally take one's life in one's arms.*
>
> —*Arthur Miller*
> After the Fall

◆ IS PAT DRIVING YOU CRAZY? ◆

Imagine you have a Siamese twin named Pat. Because your left hip is attached to Pat's right hip, it's obvious that both of you spend a lot of time together. Since you both like to drive, you buy a student driver car with dual steering wheels and pedal controls. Several years after buying the car, you suddenly realize that although you are the better driver, Pat does most of the driving. You also become aware that even when you do drive, Pat controls things by being an arrogant navigator. It seems that because Pat's head popped out of your mother first, Pat became the dominant older sibling. This is unfortunate because you have better eyesight, reflexes, judgment, and sense of direction. In addition, you have a healthier choice of destinations. In reality, Pat's success can be attributed to an overabundance of attitude, assurance, and unearned confidence.

The problem is that when Pat is driving, it is common to find yourselves in the woods, on someone's front lawn, or in a deserted drive-in movie. You once spent two days in a narrow dead-end alley because Pat was sure there was a way out other than putting the car into reverse.

One mistake you make is letting Pat drive. Pat's license should have been revoked years ago. Another mistake is trusting that Pat is driving correctly when you are watching the scenery or taking a nap. More often than not, you are frustrated and disappointed when you discover just where you wind up.

If you ever look around your own life and say, "How in the world did I ever get here?" perhaps the answer is that Pat got you there. If you feel that you would never have intentionally created the life you currently lead, your main error is putting too much trust into your out-of-control and dominant sibling. You have unwittingly entered into a collusion. Pat agrees to take over the helm while you agree to become submissive to Pat's whims, values, and phobias. The good news is that you do not have to change too many things in order to gain back command of your life.

The first skill to develop is the ability to distinguish Pat from yourself.
Below is a list to help you accomplish this.

1. Any time you compare your own skills, intelligence, wealth, and looks to someone else's, and feel better or worse, depending on how you measure up, it's Pat.

2. Whenever you attempt to control an outcome with intimidation, aggressiveness, or omission, it's Pat.

3. If you constantly complain about the same problem, situation, or bad habit, but never solve, cure, or accept it, it's Pat.

4. Whenever hopeless, impossible, or "it's too late in life" thoughts and feelings come up, it's Pat.

5. If you go around with a negative running commentary about people, places, and things, assume it's Pat.

6. Whenever you are more focused on being interesting, rather than being interested in people, it's Pat.

7. Any time you are obsessed with achieving specific results and oblivious to the price you are paying for the results, it's Pat.

8. If you find yourself more comfortable thinking and talking about the past or the future, rather than living in present time, it's Pat.

9. If it is difficult to say I'm sorry, or admit you were wrong (especially if you are a parent or head of a company), it's Pat.

10. Whenever you can't be lovingly teased, it's Pat.

11. If you have this burning desire to get the last winning word in during most arguments, it's Pat.

12. Whenever you live in a world of just black and white and have no room for shades of gray, it's Pat.

13. If you think you'll be happy only after you achieve success or reach a certain goal, it's Pat.

14. Whenever you feel you are in desperate need of a compliment, more often than not, it's Pat.

15. If you are constantly dwelling on what you don't have, it's Pat.

16. Whenever you are generating evidence or trying to keep score in a relationship (you-owe-me-one type of mentality), it's Pat.

17. If you love telling people what they should do and how they should feel, it's Pat.

18. Any time you are lecturing someone rather than sharing or communicating with them, it's Pat.

19. If you have difficulty listening to someone's side of the argument and are unable to see and hear their point of view (even if you don't agree with it), it's Pat.

20. Whenever you are terrified of losing everyone's love, it's Pat.

21. If you are constantly checking yourself out in a mirror, it's Pat.

22. Any time you trash people or gossip about them, it's Pat.

23. If you have a constant need to be the performer (by entertaining and educating) rather than the audience (by listening and learning), it's Pat.

24. If you'd love to be more successful, but you fear the process will take too much effort and cause too much struggle and pain, it's Pat's perception.

25. Whenever you feel uncomfortable around people who have more information, different opinions, and values than your own, it's usually Pat.

26. If you experience fear and terror whenever you begin something new, it's Pat.

27. If you feel safer around people after you go to the gym and pump up your muscles, it's Pat who is pumping the iron.

28. Any time you attempt to obliterate some negative aspect of your personality, it's Pat.

29. If it's easier for you to work harder rather than smarter, it's Pat.

30. If you'd rather perk yourself up by taking a cup of coffee or a cigarette, rather than a short walk around the block, a quick nap or a glass of juice, it's Pat.

31. If it is difficult for you to give or receive a compliment, it's Pat.

32. If you have very little patience (with yourself and others) and lack tolerance when you encounter any form of incompetence, it's Pat.

33. If you are always seeking answers and then dismissing every answer you receive as not the one, it's Pat.

34. If you can only operate on two speeds, one being procrastination and the other being a panic-induced productivity, it's Pat.

35. If you are always walking around overwhelmed, depressed, and annoyed at all of the commitments you've agreed to, it's Pat.

36. If whatever you accomplish is never good enough, and whatever you are currently doing is never quite *it,* the critic is Pat.

37. If you hate this list, I hate to tell you but—it's Pat.

If you find you relate to more of these statements than you'd like to admit, don't get upset. There is a lot of Pat in all of us. Once again, the most important skill to develop is the identification of Pat. This simple awareness of when you are "Patting" and when you are "Selfing" is worth its weight in gold. When I first began this isolation process, I discovered that Pat was controlling most of my life. The more aware I became of Pat, however, the easier it was for me to shift back into a selfing state.

If you want to know how to tap more into yourself and less into Pat, I would suggest you begin looking for yourself in a calm, creative, and playful part of your mind and body. Remember, whenever there is a lot of internal commotion, chatter, and critiquing, assume Pat is running the show. Here are some specific actions that can help you to focus more on yourself and less on Pat: An early-morning or late-night meditation, a walk through the woods, yoga, writing in a journal, singing, playing a sport in a joyful state, studying a martial art, holding hands with a loved one, molding clay, taking deeper and more relaxing breaths, drawing a picture, sending love into a baby's eyes, watching a sunrise or sunset, listening to or making music, feeding the homeless as you look into their appreciative eyes.

In addition, you will experience yourself more often when you are able to be with uncomfortable feelings and emotions. By being willing to experience these unpleasant sensations (when facing challenging situations) and not trying to change, numb, deny, or annihilate them, you will tap into more of yourself and less of Pat. (See "The Door Process" on page 143.)

It's also important to know that your twin has an agenda opposite to yours and rarely in your best interest. If you want to be thinner, Pat will have an enormous appetite. If you want to be more organized, Pat will be totally disorganized. Here is a more detailed example of what I'm talking about. If your dream is to write and sell a novel, Pat, seeing that this dream is already taken, will take an opposite one. Pat's dream will be to become the type of person who has plenty of talent but who never fully realizes it. To accomplish this, Pat will create obstacles, perhaps constantly blame a painful childhood, or be obsessed with a limiting disability. In addition, Pat will attract people who will help to support this perception. This will include friends who show an enormous amount of concern about poor Pat's situation. Pat will also hook up with people who will distract him or her with invitations, draining phone calls, and addictive substances. All of these people and situations will help support Pat's dream – being full of potential and possibility but never achieving tangible results.

There is an additional piece of information you need to know about Pat. Unfortunately, your twin suffers from a split personality. Schizoid Pat will give you a piece of advice and then, after you heed the advice, turn around and attack you for making that exact decision. Then, Pat will engage in a heated discussion (taking both parts). Pat will tell you to go ahead and eat that piece of pie and afterwards berate you for being so undisciplined and out of control. Pat will first tell you it's okay to hit the snooze alarm "just one more time," and then later on will curse you for once again running late. Pat will tell you that you have worked out in the gym enough and then afterwards get angry with you for not being in better shape.

The secret to weathering these Pat-to-Pat conversations is in knowing that neither position or argument is your own. Pat is parading around disguised as both the advisor and the critic. By applying The 15 Second Principle you can stop and create a little distance between youself and the voices. This will enable you to step out of the play and become a third party to these dueling Pat conversations. Once this occurs you will be freer to take back control of your life. Breck Costin, a leading Los Angeles consultant and personal coach, helps us to identify Pat with the simple yet life-altering phrase "noise or no noise." When there are constant discussions and debates going on inside your head (regardless of how brilliant), it's Pat. When there is calm, peacefulness, and serenity, it's you. It's important to know the louder the chatter and fiercer the battling in your head, the more difficult it is to take an appropriate action.

Here is a game you can play that will also help to separate you from Pat. I call it the Angel Game. What if you were actually an angel placed on earth, but you didn't realize it? Once you discovered this fact, would you still feel as vulnerable, opinionated, and intense as Pat? Once you review the Pat list you'll realize the two common denominators that run Pat's life are scarcity and insecurity. Because angels will always have everything they need, they are never threatened by loss, rushing to grab more, or racing to get somewhere. Instead, they come from security and abundance as they share and receive love. Anytime you are confused about who you are being, stop and ask yourself, "Would an angel think, feel, or behave like this?" If the answer is no, assume Pat is once again at the helm.

While it might be tempting, your objective is never to kill Pat off. If you do, you would have an enormous amount of dead weight to carry around for the rest of your life. (Recall "The Inclusion Factor" from the last section.) Instead, your goal is to keep distinguishing Pat from yourself. This is where The 15 Second Principle comes in handy. It only takes a few seconds to ask yourself, "Who's driving my car?" "Am I behaving like a babbling and petty Pat, or my angel self?"

Remember, anytime there is loud, opinionated, and critical dialoguing in your mind, assume the chatter and discourse are coming from Pat. By separating Pat from yourself, you will be much freer to redirect your attention and choose a more nurturing and mini-action mode of thinking, acting, and producing. This, in turn, will enable you to tap into your personal manifest destiny that is just waiting to be discovered.

◆ BOZO THE CHIMP ◆

Once upon a time there was a very talented chimp named Bozo, who was a retired circus performer. He lived on a deserted farm with his trainer, Joey. Bozo's greatest joy was riding a miniature motorcycle that Joey had built for him. Each morning the chimp would wake up early, dress himself, eat a banana, and juggle golf balls until Joey came downstairs. After breakfast, they'd go outside where there were thousands of acres of beautiful land.

Joey would start up Bozo's motorcycle and allow him to ride it around a circular dirt track next to the farmhouse. Bozo would ride around the track for hours at a time and would only stop when he ran out of gas. Each day, the chimp would log on hundreds of miles as he raced around this sixteenth-of-a-mile track. Neighbors loved looking out their windows to see Bozo enjoying himself by racing around the dirt track.

After a few years of this ritual, the chimp's favorite neighbor, Ralph, a retired banana wholesaler, realized something interesting was going on. When he glanced out his window, although he could still see an enormous amount of dust being kicked up into the air, he couldn't see Bozo or his motorcycle. When he walked over to take a closer look, he discovered that over the years Bozo's motorcycle had carved a six-foot-deep circular trench out of the track. Ralph located Bozo as he was racing round the bend of the sunken track. Bozo was wearing goggles, a leather chin-strapped cap, and was entirely covered with dust. He was smiling, coughing, and wheezing. Ralph began to laugh, knowing that this poor chimp was making great time going nowhere.

Had Bozo experimented with straightening out his handlebars (while still maintaining his balance), the chimp would have had options other than going around and around in one small circle. With this additional skill, some courage, and curiosity, Bozo could have explored many different areas of town.

Perhaps there is a little of Bozo in all of us. We get so caught up in our familiar patterns and limiting conversations that at some point these habits become closed loops limiting our progress and creativity. While we can expend a lot of energy, we will reap few new results other than digging deeper ruts into the same old terrain. The purpose of The 15 Second Principle is to encourage you to change any constraining or bankrupt behavior (regularly berating yourself for lateness, for example, yet never actually breaking the pattern, is bankrupt behavior). By straightening out the handlebars of your life you will be able to break out of a circular arena of limiting familiarity and into a spacious yet unfamiliar realm of wonder, risk, and daring. It's interesting to note that one definition of madness is always taking the same actions while expecting different results.

Whenever you suspect that you are "looping," stop and apply The 15 Second Principle. Remind yourself that at every moment of every day there are many choices available to you. Are you going to select the same old, comfortable, yet confining choice or are you going to get courageous and take a different approach? Can you execute any mini-action that will allow you to "de-Bozo" yourself? Can you move any chess piece in your life a little differently? Is there a phone call you can make? Is there one pushup you can do? Is there one drink or cigarette you can *not* take? Any mini-action that you can perform will serve as a valuable "de-looping" technique. This, in turn, will create more spontaneity, freedom, vitality, and choice in every area of your life.

> *Most people live, whether physically, intellectually, or morally, in a very restricted circle of their potential being. They make use of a very small portion of their possible consciousness, and of their soul's resources in general, much like a man who, out of his whole bodily organism, should get into a habit of using and moving only his little finger.*

> *Great emergencies and crises show us how much greater*
> *our vital resources are than we had supposed.*

> —*William James*

◆ GOING INTO RECEIVERSHIP ◆

Do rich, successful, and lucky people possess a skill that poor, unsuccessful, and unlucky people do not have? I believe the answer is yes. For most, that magical trait is their ability *to receive*. They are ready and willing to receive success. On a conscious and/or unconscious level, they are open and available for it to occur. It's not enough to be smart and to work hard. It's not enough to be a wonderful and caring person. It's not enough to have a plan and a goal. You must also have the magnetic capacity to receive the rewards, joys, and riches that the planet can provide.

Have you ever met a woman who is successful, yet never seems to be struggling to close deals? Somehow, clients, customers, and deals just seem to appear at her doorstep. Did you go to school with a guy who wasn't very bright, then find out that he's now a multimillionaire? Have you ever met a woman who wasn't beautiful, yet always seemed to attract handsome and eligible men? Have you ever met a guy who was rude and crude, yet lived like a king on a mountaintop?

Perhaps the common denominator here is their ability to receive. People who have mastered this receivership skill don't have guilt or negative feelings associated with concepts such as prosperity, money, and power. Neither do they have sabotaging mechanisms built into their unconscious. For right reasons or wrong ones, they feel comfortable with the concepts of receiving and abundance.

The ability to receive is the fundamental building block for all success. Developing this receiving muscle is a crucial element to master. Here are some helpful actions that can expand your ability to receive.

Breathe Consciously

The simple act of conscious breathing is a very dynamic action. With each inhalation you can rediscover the wonders of receiving the greatest gift of all: air. This most basic act will constantly remind you of your right to receive. The more aware you become of your breathing patterns (shallow or deep, fast or slow), the stronger your receivership capacity will become. Each inhalation offers an opportunity to take in feelings of love and self-worth.

Many people, when they encounter something or someone they feel they don't deserve to have or to know, will respond by unconsciously holding their breath. This bracing or freezing will prevent any receivership and spontaneity from occurring. To counterbalance this tendency, become more aware of your breathing patterns. Make sure you are receiving air when you meet a beautiful person, see a luxurious car, and pass a magnificent home. Your receivership breath will remind you that you deserve to have it all.

Exhaling will remind you to share more of what you already have. Exhale your love and generosity. This action can also assist you in releasing any excess tension, exhaustion, or fear. It is helpful to let the air out naturally rather than aggressively forcing it out. In your breathing, as well as your life, what you are after is a harmonious relationship between receiving and giving. (See "Scuba Breathing on Land" on page 150 for a full discussion of conscious breathing.)

Have a Worthy Reason

Another way to enhance your receivership ability is to have a worthy reason to receive. If your skill of receiving is weak, find a purpose that is larger than your own self-interest. Pick a cause or charity that you believe in. Promise to donate a portion of your time or future income to this goal or organization. Be as generous as you can with the percentage. The more you can stretch in this area, the better. Make this agreement even if you are penniless or in debt. From a metaphysical standpoint, this sharing contract will set up a powerful magnetic field. It will form an attraction recipe that will improve the chances to receive.

Learn to Let Go

Believe it or not, in order to improve your capacity to receive, you must also strengthen your ability to lose. Many people hate the feeling of losing or giving up anything. This even includes abusive relationships, cluttered rooms, and stale memories. If given a choice, our old friend Homeostasis will choose familiarity over newness. However, in order to grow, change, and receive, you must accept initial loss as part of the package.

Physicists tell us that the universe loves to fill any vacuum. If the universe has already taken this filling job, then what is your task? Your job is first to create the vacuum. This can be accomplished by an emptying-out process. The clearer the space, the more powerful the suction of the vacuum. The great part of this process is that you only have to know *what isn't working in your life.* Your assignment is to look around for the clutter and addictions and then be brave enough to let go of them. This includes draining and distracting relationships, valuable clothing that you never wear, brilliant books and articles that you know you will never have time to read, and inherited furniture that you never loved in the first place.

The space you create will help to attract other opportunities. If you find this isn't the case, one of two things is happening. Either you are not specific enough in declaring or you are still emotionally attached to a person, place, or thing that you thought you were free from. If attachment is the issue, what's called for is a releasing process. Sometimes writing a good-bye completion letter will help you disengage from these lingering feelings. The letter doesn't have to be mailed, and it can even address a person who is deceased or an old flame you haven't seen in decades. Remember, this clearing of the space and acceptance of the pangs of loss will ultimately enable you to experience the joys of gain.

Remember the Umbrella

Here is a physical exercise that will help you to expand your ability to receive. Take one of those large, old-fashioned umbrellas.

Make sure it has a long tip at the end. Take the umbrella outside, open it, and hold it as you normally would. Now imagine you are in a dry, hot desert and you are literally dying of thirst. You are using the umbrella to protect yourself from the blistering sun. Suddenly, it begins to get cloudy and then to rain. How are you going to use the umbrella now? Rather than trying to protect yourself from getting wet, you will turn the umbrella upside down and use its long tip as a makeshift handle. In this manner you will catch as much rain as the umbrella will hold. This inversion action will convert a protective shield into a receptive reservoir.

One of the secrets of receivership is to walk through life with an invisible inverted umbrella. This image will constantly remind you of your God-given right to receive in abundance. Unfortunately, most of us walk through life with a protective upright umbrella that prevents anything from reaching us.

*   *   *

It's important to remember that there is nothing wrong or greedy about the desire to receive. As long as there are pockets of wealth on the planet, why shouldn't you work toward receiving a portion of them? Philanthropists have to develop their ability to receive before they can have anything in their bank accounts to share. The larger our reservoir, the more it can hold and the more generous we can be with our neighbors. Let's remember Scrooge's lesson. The greatest joy of all comes from sharing. Ebenezer was leading a miserable and meaningless life collecting money until he began to share his wealth, time, and heart with the rest of the village.

Whenever we feel that our life is not going the way we want it to be going, rather than looking outward and blaming external circumstances, we need to look inward. The 15 Second Principle can help us to stop and do some internal soul-searching. Most of the time, what is standing between us and our dreams is ourselves.

A cautionary word is necessary here. History reveals that those who experience the most satisfaction from receiving are those who have put in their dues by working diligently toward a goal. Executives who build up their own companies report more satisfaction than lottery winners. Students who write their own papers receive more satisfaction and feel more self-worth than those who plagiarize. People who earn their income usually experience more enjoyment spending it than people who have inherited it. Apparently, the more creative and involved we become in the process of receiving, the greater our satisfaction. The secret, then, is to feel that you deserve to receive, to expand your capacity to receive, and then to work in a committed fashion to fulfill your passionate mission.

◆ THE ART OF WEDGING ◆

The art of wedging is about separating ourselves from our old and limiting beliefs. It is also about freeing ourselves from inertia, fear, and restrictive behavior. By gently placing a wedge between ourselves and our confining thoughts and patterns, we can produce more freedom and opportunities for ourselves. This disassociation will enable us to discover more of our gifts and allow us to realize more of our dreams.

To understand the art of wedging, it will be helpful to go back in time to when people were using record players and listening to these big round black vinyl things called albums. Back to a time when the artwork on a record jacket really meant something. Recall that the record player had a large spindle that could hold many albums at one time. After the first album played, the spindle would automatically drop the second one on top of the first, and then a third one on top of the second.

Imagine now that you've got very unique records stacked on your player. They do not need a needle to be played. Instead, as soon as each record is dropped, all the songs on the record will begin to play simultaneously. If there are many albums revolving on the turntable the listener will hear a lot of noise and confusion, but little music.

Let's say that there is already an album playing on your turntable. It is called *My Freedom and My Potential.* This is your personal album of unlimited potentiality, where anything is possible. On it is only one song, called "My Wonderful Life."

Now picture a second album falling on the first. It is entitled *The "Truths" of My Family* a.k.a. *The Things I Bought for Free*. This album echoes the fears and concerns you hear – or heard – from your family, which you have internalized. On it are cuts such as: "It Is Better to Be Practical than Passionate," "The Bigger You Think, the Larger the Disappointment," "Life Is a Serious Matter," "I'm the Dumbest One in the Family," "Who Do You Think You Are?" "The Safest Place to Keep a Dream Is in the Closet," and "If Your Genius Isn't Discovered before Age Five, It Ain't There."

Let's say that now a third record falls on the second. It is entitled *Society's Values and Fears*. On it are such classics as "More Is Better," "The Only Thing Separating Me from Happiness Is a Little More Money," "You'll Never Be OK without a Mercedes," "Another Economic Depression Could Be around the Corner," and "If You Are Not Gorgeous, Thin, or Rich, You Might as Well Give Up."

The problem here is that the beautiful song on the first album, called "My Wonderful Life," is being drowned out and interfered with by all of the confining lyrics of the songs that are simultaneously playing from albums two and three. Because you are only human, you are quite susceptible to the limiting themes that are vying for your attention. Ultimately, the messages of all three albums can get so blended together that it becomes extremely difficult to distinguish your own truths and dreams from the pressures, values, and expectations surrounding you.

The skill is in being able to place a symbolic wedge between your album and the others. This wedge will help you to pry the other distracting albums off your precious album. While you can't destroy these other records, they at least can be raised off your album and placed back up the long spindle where they can barely be heard. This disengagement will provide more stillness, spaciousness, and solitude for your personal song to be playing. With less interference, you will be able to create more freedom and opportunities for yourself to discover just what your values, beliefs, and dreams truly are.

The art of wedging is really about self-manifest destiny. When you have a limiting thought about yourself, your life, or your future, stop and declare a time-out. Apply The 15 Second Principle by separating your album from everyone else's. Also, attempt to discover the source of this restraining message. Was it originally on your album, or were you infected by it from the contaminating messages revolving above? Once you can decipher its owner and origin, you will be freer to choose the theme as your own reality or to ignore it as someone else's protective misconception.

The art of wedging will give you the option to no longer be influenced by someone else's restricting beliefs. It will facilitate you in distinguishing personal, empowering songs from impersonal, confining ones. This uncoupling will help you achieve more goals and satisfaction with less stress and struggle.

CONTAINERIZATION

Have you ever tried pouring a full quart of milk into a thimble? I'm sure the answer is no. Your reason would be that once the thimble got full, the milk would simply spill over onto the floor. Obviously, the thimble is too small a container to hold a full quart of milk. In order to hold more of the liquid, the thimble would have to be expanded or exchanged for a larger vessel.

A similar phenomenon occurs in life. The mind has the capacity to create different-sized visionary containers. If it creates a small container for itself, as happens with low self-esteem, and a large and empowering thought or opportunity arrives, due to the limited capacity of the vessel we would be unable to take advantage of it. It would be uncontainable. As a result, we would not be able to entertain this as a new possibility. This is why low self-esteem is such a disabling "dis-ease." It limits the mind's capacity to hold and be comfortable with big plans, passionate dreams, and dynamic conversation. This confining self-concept vessel will prevent us from ever realizing our full potential, regardless of our education, talent, or energy.

Here is a powerful process to help children (and adults) experience and emotionalize the above concept. First, look around the house for three different-sized empty containers, without lids.

An empty quart-sized milk carton, a gallon can, and a pail or wastebasket will be perfect. Next, find a large, uninflated balloon. The balloon represents our full potential and the different containers represent the limits of our self-concept.

Place the uninflated balloon inside each container and have your child attempt to blow it up. He or she will instantly experience that the larger the container, the larger the balloon will be allowed to expand. The balloon stands for who we really are and what we ultimately can do and become. The containers represent our self-entitlements and self-doubts. Unfortunately, a small container will restrict our ability to receive. A large container, on the other hand, will allow more possibility in every area of our lives.

The challenge is to expand the containers that are inside our heads. Just as people go to the gym to build up their muscles, so must we visit our mental gym to enlarge our self-entitlement containers. Sometimes our identity vessel can become so old, brittle, and rigid that in order to expand our container, we must symbolically abandon our old self-image. Just as the snake sheds its skin and the caterpillar turns into a butterfly, so must we discard a familiar yet restricting self-identity. (This requires us to trust and risk that we won't disappear or die.) As the philospher and physician Maxwell Maltz reminds us, by expanding the self-image we can expand "the area of the possible."

The most important thing to realize about the containerization process is that our identity balloon is much more supple, expandable, and resilient than we think. Although we may feel that it is fragile and small, most of the time this is just not the case. Our identity balloon is in fact huge, vibrant, durable, and just waiting to expand. Ultimately, we want to be free of all containers. Once this occurs, our identity balloon will keep expanding to its rightful size and unique shape. It's inspiring to note that Auguste Rodin, the brilliant French sculptor, believed that our mission in life was to grow ourselves into what we were really meant to be.

Any time you feel unable to risk and expand, stop and apply The 15 Second Principle. Take a little time to discover where these limiting feelings and thoughts are emanating from. More often than not, they are coming from a confining container and not an expansive balloon of potentiality. A confining container is usually created by the incorrect lies that we bought into (from early childhood and family experiences), the obsolete fears that still rule us, and the false and fearful perceptions that incorrectly color our world. While a limited container may feel like our deepest truth, in fact it is not. A powerful question to ask ourselves is, If I believe and feel my container to be smaller than it is in fact, where in my life did I get this perception? Most of the time the answer can be found in the dynamics of the family, a close friend, or a teacher.

It's also difficult to shed a limiting container because we often get a lot of emotional mileage out of it. Acting and feeling as if we have a small container provides a safe identity. It also generates a lot of love, concern, and attention. Many families and friendships create relationships that are built around this dynamic. Sometimes, in order to create a larger identity vessel, we must be courageous and risk losing the attention and love that we are currently receiving. In a sense, we have to risk losing other people's love and risk how other people perceive and relate to us in order to gain more of our own love and self-worth. This can be a frightening experience that calls for an enormous amount of courage and faith.

However, by facing this fear and stretching our self-entitlement container, we can realize even more of our latent potentiality. Nelson Mandela brilliantly captures the spirit of the concept in his 1994 inaugural speech:

> *Our deepest fear is not that we are inadequate. Our deepest fear is that we are powerful beyond measure. It is our light, not our darkness, that frightens us. We ask ourselves, who am I to be brilliant, gorgeous, talented and fabulous? Actually, who are you not to be? You are a child of God. Your playing small doesn't serve the world. There's nothing enlightened about shrinking so that other people won't feel insecure around you. We were born to make manifest the glory of God that is within us. It's not just in some of us; it's in everyone. And as we let our own light shine, we unconsciously give other people permission to do the same. As we are liberated from our own fear, our presence automatically liberates others.*

◄EXPANDING YOUR BOUNDARIES►

*When we can gather the courage and take one
more step beyond our perceived limits, what we will
discover is that there is still ground beneath our feet.*

—*Al Secunda*

When we were young, our parents, relatives, older siblings, teachers, and baby-sitters created protective boundaries for us. For our
own well-being, they told us where it was safe and unsafe to venture. We were told such things as "You can go as far as the tree,
but no farther. You can walk up to the corner, but never cross the
street. Don't go near the water. Don't talk to strangers. Never
leave the classroom without taking the pass." While all of these
commands were meant for our own safety and security, they inad-
vertently also planted boundary seeds in our unconscious minds.
As we got older, these limiting seeds matured into powerful
weeds whose restraining messages still echo somewhere inside us.

The best way to grasp the power of this early restrictive programming is to view it in animals. In Deepak Chopra's *Magical
Mind, Magical Body* audio series, we find the following two examples of boundary indoctrinations.

How to Train an Elephant

*1. In India, people train elephants in a fascinating manner. They take
baby elephants and place a thick chain around one of their front legs.
Next, they attach the chain to the base of a large tree. The little elephant
quickly surrenders and does not try to venture past the length of the chain.
Here's where the story gets interesting. As the elephant grows and becomes
larger and stronger, the trainers replace the thick chain with thinner and
thinner ones. They also attach these chains to smaller and smaller trees.
Eventually, a thin piece of rope connects the elephant to a small tree.
While the elephant now has the strength to snap the rope or to uproot the
entire tree with its trunk, it does not. Instead, it chooses to perceive and
react to the rope and tree as though they were the original thick chain*

and strong anchor. The adult elephant relates to its current world through its past and limited reality.

How to Separate Fish

2. *Scientists conducted a revealing experiment with tropical fish. They partitioned a fish tank by lowering a piece of glass into the center of the tank. They arbitrarily put half the fish in one section and half in the other section. After some time the scientists removed the glass partition. Interestingly enough, what they discovered was that none of the fish ventured across into the other section of the tank. They became so "comfortable" in their limited little world that they were still honoring the partition, even when it was removed. Their conditioning stifled their mobility and curiosity. Apparently, they did not feel safe visiting an unfamiliar neighborhood.*

*   *   *

Old realities and obsolete beliefs often can limit and negatively affect our new adventures and endeavors. Directly or indirectly, they diminish the *permission* we give ourselves to venture past our familiar boundaries. These habits in turn determine just how far we are able to stretch our own personal envelopes. While old convictions and beliefs might have once acted as shields that protected us, at some point they usually turn into barricades that restrict us.

Take a minute to dwell on the following question: Which areas in your life are you giving yourself permission to play in, and which areas are off-limits to you? More specifically, Which job are you afraid to apply for? Which exercise or diet program are you afraid to begin? What course are you afraid to sign up for? Which city are you afraid to visit or move to? Which potential customer or romantic interest are you afraid to call? What article are you afraid to write? What large sum of money are you afraid to make?

Many people, after asking themselves the above questions, discover that they have a lot in common with elephants and fish. Unfortunately, early programming and unsuccessful adventures are still keeping a lot of us locked up in the same zoo.

To counterbalance these limiting tendencies, start becoming more aware of your habits and behavior. Become an observant witness to your patterns and fears. This will help you determine whether your fears are deciding your future or whether you are free to choose the future that is locked up inside of you and dying to get out.

When making your observations, be sure they are nonjudgmental in nature. Rather than labeling something as bad, refer to it as *interesting*. "That's interesting how I can never seem to call that CEO." "That's interesting how even though I'm attracted to Chris, I can't seem to make eye contact and say hello." "It's interesting that I love to go bicycle riding, yet I never schedule time for it." "It's interesting how I'm fascinated by psychology, yet I never signed up for any classes in it."

The more *conscious yet neutral* you can become in your observations, the less power these limiting habits and phobias will have over you. By becoming more aware of your patterns they will begin to control you less. This, in turn, will enable you to choose a more passionate, rewarding, and courageous path. In truth, if we had the power to invent these self-imposed boundaries, then we also have the power to do away with them.

Another important element in this freeing process is to stop complaining about the behavior you want to change. Rather than motivating you, the complaint, whether you make it verbally or physically (through body language), will lock you into the unwanted behavior. If you can't stop the behavior, then at least stop complaining about it. A complaint is a mini-addiction that feeds and keeps the unwanted behavior in place. By stopping the habit of complaining, you will at least begin to change some aspect of this pattern. This alone will improve your chances of releasing yourself from the unwanted behavior.

A perfect conclusion to this boundary discussion is the following inspirational message. Published in Ram Dass's *Journey of Awakening*, it was written by Nadine Stair, a woman from Louisville, Kentucky, who at the time was eighty-five years old.

If I Had My Life to Live Over

I'd like to make more mistakes next time. I'd relax. I would limber up. I would be sillier than I have been this trip. I would take fewer things seriously. I would take more chances. I would climb more mountains and swim more rivers. I would eat more ice cream and less beans. I would perhaps have more actual troubles, but I'd have fewer imaginary ones.

You see, I'm one of those people who live sensibly and sanely hour after hour, day after day. Oh, I've had my moments, and if I had it to do over again, I'd have more of them. In fact, I'd try to have nothing else. Just moments, one after another, instead of living so many years ahead of each day. I've been one of those persons who never goes anywhere without a thermometer, a hot water bottle, a raincoat, and a parachute. If I had to do it again, I would travel lighter than I have.

If I had my life to live over, I would start barefoot earlier in the spring and stay that way later in the fall. I would go to more dances. I would ride more merry-go-rounds. I would pick more daisies.

HOW TO CHANGE A HABIT

*Habit is habit, and not to be flung out
of the window, but coaxed downstairs
a step at a time.*

—*Mark Twain*

It appears that while most of us would love to change some aspect of our lives, many of us do not have the necessary discipline or tools to accomplish this wish. As a result, each time we attempt to alter our behavior, we come up short. From changing our eating habits to starting an exercise regimen, from stopping smoking to getting ourselves more organized, from improving our financial situation to changing our sleeping and waking habits, many of us do not succeed.

Before we begin discussing a success strategy for change, we first need to define two terms: *charged behavior* and *uncharged behavior*.

Charged behavior encompasses all the habits that we are aware of and that we want to change. We place negative emotional value on these habits. Some examples of charged behavior might be eating the wrong foods, smoking, procrastinating, waking up too late in the morning, drinking too much, biting our nails, or being disorganized.

Uncharged behavior includes all the patterns that we may or may not be aware of, but that are not important to us. As a result, we don't care much about changing them. Some examples of uncharged behavior might be using our dominant arm and hand to perform many chores (dialing the phone, opening drawers, carrying objects), getting into bed and dropping our socks on the floor, and squeezing the toothpaste tube a certain way.

One of the main reasons we have difficulty changing patterns is that most of us do not know how to approach them. What most of us do is to leave most everything in our lives the same and single out the one charged behavior we want to change. We attempt to change this behavior by getting serious, focused, and aggressively attacking it. What we neglect to realize is that Homeostasis is very attached to and protective of charged behavior. As a result, more often than not Homeostasis rallies to the rescue and does a heroic job of fending off the new behavior.

Instead, before changing a charged behavior it is best to alter some harmless uncharged behaviors first. We want to reassure Homeostasis that just because we are changing some habits, it doesn't necessarily mean that Homeo should get activated and switch into a defensive and protective mode.

Sharon's Desire to Change

Let's use a fictional character named Sharon to illustrate an effective course of action for building on a desire to change. Sharon is a very tall, attractive, and successful account executive who wants to lose twenty pounds. Before she begins to lose the weight (a charged behavior), she should first do a few other things. First, she should attempt to change her relationship with her weight. While she'd prefer to be thinner, the excess pounds should not become the enemy that she is attacking. Up until this moment, the weight may have even served some emotional purpose. Two good questions for Sharon to be dwelling on are: "What purpose is this extra weight serving?" and "What would I be giving up if I let go of [rather than lost] this weight?" Is her extra weight serving as a protective shield? If so, is she now willing to release it? Is her excessive eating to fill up an emotional emptiness? If so, is she now willing to experience and explore that feeling of emptiness?

In addition, has Sharon's constant weight complaining (silently and vocally) become an invisible sub-addiction? Is she at least willing to begin by giving up the pattern of complaining and berating herself about her eating habits and weight? Oftentimes it's the constant complaining that keeps the unwanted pattern or characteristic locked in place.

Next, Sharon should become more aware of her life patterns and daily uncharged behaviors. If her life were videotaped for a week (morning through night) and later played back for her, she would begin to see recurring themes (physical, verbal, and emotional). Sharon might observe the following:

Actions

- When entering the bathroom in the morning, she always turns the light on with her left hand.

- When picking up the phone, she usually uses her right hand.

- When putting on her socks, panty hose, or jeans, she always starts with her left foot.

- When opening the silverware drawer in the kitchen, she usually uses her left hand.

- When carrying a shoulder bag, she usually hangs it over her right shoulder.

- When speaking on the phone she frequently says, "You know what I mean?"

• When talking to men she usually twirls her hair with her right hand.

The first week, Sharon's main assignment is just to become an *objective witness* to her own actions and patterns (both charged and uncharged). She should apply The 15 Second Principle several times a day by observing her actions and making mental or written lists of her discoveries.

The second week, Sharon's assignment is to change at least one of her old, uncharged behaviors each day. For example, Sharon will now always open the silverware drawer with her right hand; she will now carry her shoulder bag over her left shoulder. Within a week, Sharon's goal is to change permanently seven of her uncharged behaviors.

The third week, Sharon will start to follow a few aspects of her medically sound weight-loss program. She may have one less piece of toast. She may take a little more salad, less dressing, and fewer rolls. At least once a day, she takes the staircase instead of the elevator. Whenever she walks, she will lengthen her stride and pick up her pace. Not yet strictly following her new health program, Sharon slowly starts going toward it.

The fourth week, Sharon becomes a little more committed to following additional aspects of her eating and exercising program.

The fifth week, Sharon is following most of the program.

The sixth week Sharon is fully committed to her program.

Whenever Sharon has a setback with her eating agreements, she increases her awareness of why this occurred, forgives herself, and immediately returns to one of the above weekly programs. It doesn't really matter which weekly program she returns to. Sharon must keep reminding herself that this is an ongoing process and personal journey, not a grueling "stopwatch" race with a finite finishing line. What is most important is that if she falters, she must forgive herself and reenroll somewhere back into the six-week program. Ultimately Sharon's apparently long, six-week mini-action approach will turn out to be a fast shortcut to health, balance, and mastery.

Keep remembering that the secret to changing charged behavior
is first to alter uncharged behavior. In addition, whenever you
have your eye too far down the road, stop and apply The 15
Second Principle. Remind yourself that a slow and steady process
is the name of the mastery game. This slow and steady process will
sustain your momentum, strengthen your stamina, and improve
the odds that Homeostasis will not stand in the way of desired
change.

Our Ultimate Performance Zone

When an archer is shooting for enjoyment, he has all his skill; when he shoots for a brass buckle, he gets nervous; when he shoots for a prize of gold, he begins to see two targets.

—*Chuang Tzu*

I's late at night as I sit in the kitchen of my parents' home in Queens, New York City. In the middle of my post-midnight snack, I move the white curtains aside and peer out the window. Although it is quite dark outside, I am able to make out the shadow-infested back alley, the sight of which still evokes tales of my childhood. The memories of my early athletic experiences still seem to echo out of every corner of this makeshift playground. The cement alley served as our primitive ball field while growing up. It runs one long city block and is incredibly narrow (approximately the width of two cars). The major sporting event played in this challenging "ball park" was stickball, which is played with a cutoff broomstick and a pink rubber ball.

My first "major league" experience occurred in this alley when I was only six years old. I was drafted by the "big boys" (ages eight through twelve) when one of their regulars, Big Barry, didn't show up. Their hardest decision was to find a position for me where I'd do the least damage. They finally decided to create a special position for me called the "out" outfield. In this location, I had two jobs. The first was to back up our only outfielder. The second was to help retrieve dozens of foul balls. Because the alley was so long and narrow, very few balls ever stayed fair once they got to the outfield. Instead, most of them would wind up under some neighbor's rose bush or on a brick back porch.

I can still remember being delighted about my "out" outfield assignment because I knew it would be very difficult for me to screw up. During the first half of the game, I got to stop one ground ball and found several foul balls. Then, in the ninth inning, with two men on base, Jay Wanderman came up to bat and hit a powerful fly ball. The thing kept sailing higher and higher, deeper and deeper, and, unfortunately for me, straighter and straighter. It was obvious that this ball had no intention of going foul. As it flew over the outfielder's head, I knew I was in trouble. As everyone's attention turned to me, I quickly moved backwards, opened my panic-stricken eyes, held my breath, raised my stiff arms in the air, and, with frozen fingers, miraculously caught the ball. Everyone, including me, was shocked at the outcome. I was a hero for an hour.

In retrospect, this very successful catching experience turned out to be the most counterproductive event of my life. I say this because by catching the ball in this panic-stricken and finger-frozen manner, I got the unintended message that terror and tension could help me to achieve results. Is it any wonder then that I unconsciously used this prescription for success when taking exams, hitting tennis balls, writing reports, and playing difficult passages on the flute?

Had I dropped the ball instead, perhaps I would have realized that terror and tension would not produce an ultimate performance zone. I then could have looked in areas other than stiffness, fright, and survival when attempting to achieve results. I might have experimented with relaxation, trust, and enjoyment as vital ingredients to a more ideal performing state. Instead, I went through a few decades never understanding that I was sitting on a lot of buried talent. It wasn't until my early thirties that I realized that this bracing-to-perform mentality was affecting my entire world.

By becoming more conscious of my tension-filled habits and obsolete belief systems, I was able to build a more efficient performance zone. Learning how to create from a more open and relaxed place requires patience, faith, and practice. This is especially true if you are achieving respectable results with your current behavior. In such cases, you will be unaware that there are even more enjoyable and efficient ways to realize your goals.

From catching a falling bar of soap in the shower, to writing a report; from closing a sales deal, to speaking in front of an audience – there are ways to perform more efficiently. By applying The 15 Second Principle (in some cases it's more like 15 nanoseconds), and choosing a more effective place to produce from, the pursuit of excellence will be more inspiring and the outcomes more successful. By embracing more and bracing less, by nurturing more and stressing less, we will have an easier time discovering just how gifted we truly are.

> *According to contemporary accounts, young Christian Heinrich Heinekin, the Infant of Lubec, talked within a few hours of his birth, learned Latin, French, history and geography by age three and predicted his own death at the age of four, possibly from exhaustion.*

—*John Briggs*
Fire in the Crucible

◆ THE 15 SECOND PLEASURE PRIORITY ◆

As we go about our daily routines, we execute hundreds of tasks. We make the bed, go shopping, write checks, take exams, prepare meals, make love, close deals, drive cars, swing racquets and clubs – the list is endless. At some point in our lives, however, *how* we are doing something must become just as important as what we are doing. There should be an enjoyable and efficient manner in which we approach excellence. Even when we apply The 15 Second Principle, there should be a way to value one 15 second block of time over another.

When a master says, "I performed better today than yesterday," what is he talking about? What constitutes a better performance and what would an ultimate performance look like? First, let's define what I mean by a performance. Whenever we execute a task and we care about the result, it is a performance. If I attempt to throw a peach pit into a wastebasket that is ten feet away and I care about the results, this is a performance. However, if I am walking along a trail and toss a peach pit into the woods and don't really care where it lands, this is not a performance.

One of the goals of this book is to help people create more ultimate performances. For something to be judged an ultimate performance, it must contain two essential elements: the pleasure priority and precision.

The Pleasure Priority

The pleasure priority contains four ingredients: relaxation, energy, focus, and faith. Ideally, an ultimate performance requires all four of these ingredients. We want our bodies to be in an open and self-expressive state. We want to be in a positive, up-energy mode rather than a negative, down-energy mode (at least during the actual performance). We want all of our attention placed on executing specific actions. We want to feel that the outcome has already occurred and it is successful; hence we are able to perform in a relaxed and doubtless state.

What makes this so challenging is that consciously or unconsciously many people feel that the pleasure priority ingredients are luxuries rather than vital elements to their performing technique. They will therefore never choose the pleasure priority in emergency or potentially stressful situations. Instead, they will be suspect of it, and revert to the more familiar states of tension, seriousness, and doubt in order to produce results. This is unfortunate because when we are in a relaxed, energized, focused, and faithing mode, we are freer to access more of our talent, skills, and intuition as we act and react to the stimuli around us.

Precision

From a result-oriented standpoint, the ultimate performance should also be precise and at some point measurable. Precision is about progress and results. An ultimate performance is about increasing the chances of being a double winner—of having a wonderful time while hitting our targets. The problem with focusing too heavily on precision, however, is that it will tend to negate the pleasure priority and promote the use of tension, seriousness, and doubt as a means of producing results. This, in turn, will restrict our freedom, experience, potential, and outcomes.

For most of us, mastering the pleasure priority (relaxation, energy, focus, and faith) is the most challenging aspect of any performing or living technique. Can we still be counted on to trust the pleasure priority when our survival mechanisms are being activated? What we are talking about here is a way of being and a place to produce from when the circumstances aren't ideal, the pressure is on, and our addictions are screaming for relief. When it counts the most, where do we go in our bodies to create results? Throughout this chapter, we will continue this discussion as we keep exploring the nuances of an ultimate performance.

THE PLEASURE MODE

Whenever we perform any task or action, the experience will be either relaxed or tense, and the results will be either precise or imprecise. Therefore, each and every time we attempt to sell a product, hit a ball, give a speech, or take an exam, our experience of the act and the outcome combine in one of four distinct ways.

Chart A
Performance Possibilities Using a Goal-Oriented,
Limited Approach

EXPERIENCE	RESULTS
1) Relaxed	Precise
2) Tense	Precise
3) Relaxed	Imprecise
4) Tense	Imprecise

When we have a goal-oriented approach to our performance, we tend to value the experience/result combination in the order shown in chart A. We prefer, for example, to achieve precise results even if we are tense during the experience (the second possibility). Obviously, too, a relaxed/precise performance is more advantageous than a tense/imprecise one. The challenge is learning how to create more of these relaxed/precise experiences on a regular basis. While this is easy to talk about, accomplishing it is a completely different matter. Whenever the stakes and pressure get high, most of us consciously or unconsciously revert to tension, anxiety, and doubt in order to produce results. We choose a tightening or clutching mode of behavior rather than a pleasure priority mode. We operate out of survival rather than self-expression. While in this pressure-filled and fearful state, we do not trust the pleasure priority mode. Instead, we revert to an obsolete performance behavior of tension, fear, and doubt to bail us out. Unfortunately, these responses only limit our ability to perform well under pressure.

Relaxation versus Tension

The cosmic performing joke is that often the survival performing recipe that we automatically revert to is the very thing that is limiting and exhausting us. What is required here is a huge amount of courage. We must be willing to take a risky and dangerous leap of faith. This must occur without any visible evidence that this approach will work. Tensing and hoping must be replaced by relaxing and faithing.

I am not suggesting that you abandon your goals. Rather, I am offering an alternative approach that will help you to realize more of your objectives with greater satisfaction and ease. The best way to accomplish this is for the pleasure priority to take precedence over the precision. For this to occur you must value a relaxed, imprecise performance more than a tense, precise performance. To accomplish this you must give up your burning desire for a successful outcome. Detoxing yourself off of these instant results will require an enormous amount of commitment and character. You must be more interested in producing pleasurable and specific actions in present time and less concerned with past failures or future results. Your mission is just to live and create with relaxation, energy, focus, and faith. In this masterful state, there is no past or future. There is just creating in the now.

Afterward, you can step back and determine whether your plea-sure-priority creation was precise or imprecise. This witnessing must occur afterward. Remember, it is impossible to do your best work when you are simultaneously being the creator and the critic. Our bodies were not designed to perform well in a creator/critic straddling mode.

Chart B
Performance Possibilities Using a Process-Oriented, Limitless Approach

EXPERIENCE	RESULTS
1) Relaxed	Precise
2) Relaxed	Imprecise
3) Tense	
4) Tense	Imprecise

Performing above the Line

When we take a process-oriented, rather than a goal-oriented, approach to our performance – when we value the experience more than the re-sults – the four possible experience/result out-comes become acceptable to us in the order shown in chart B. In our pursuit of an ultimate performance, then, we must discipline ourselves always to perform above the line drawn between the second and third items. Although precision will come and go, the pleasure priority (of relaxation, energy, focus, and faith) will al-ways be constant. It's interesting to note that Wayne Gretzky, probably the greatest hockey player of all time, has a routine of purposely missing his first practice shot at the goal. He always sends the puck wide. It appears he wants to find the feeling of total freedom and self-expression in a result-free environment before ever adding precision to his shooting mix.

Regardless of the circumstances or possible outcomes, the challenge is to operate from a free, trusting, and open place. Living totally in present time will require an enormous amount of discipline, commitment, and permission. Ultimately, you must learn to value a pleasure-priority payoff (in experiential terms) above a precision-oriented result. If you begin living your life with this value system, at some point the pleasure priority (relaxation, energy, focus, and faith) will organically replace tension, fear, and doubt as your emergency performing security blanket.

What I am suggesting is that you try to control only and take responsibility for only the things that you actually can control.

- You can't guarantee that someone is going to buy your product, but you can control your mood, attitude, and feelings during a sales pitch.

- You can't know for sure who is going to win your tennis or golf match, but you can control your breathing patterns, the tension of your fingers, and your "faithing muscle" each time you swing the racquet or club.

- You can't be sure that you are going to sing the right note, but you can control the relaxation, energy, focus, and "faithing" of your body when you begin to create and experience the note.

Choosing the pleasure priority as a way of life is a very challenging mission, especially if you are competitive and perfectionistic. Demanding people tend to value results, the score, and their reputations more than the actual experience of the performance or the "cost" to their bodies. The problem with using excessive pressure, tension, and anxiety to fuel your performance is that your productivity will be survival-driven. With survival-induced adrenaline motivating you, you will be producing from terror rather than self-expression and trust. Ultimately, this type of approach will take its toll on your body, mind, and soul.

The easiest way to develop your pleasure priority is by first placing yourself in less competitive and pressurized situations. In a nondemanding setting, it will be easier to create the necessary pleasurable grading system for yourself. Each time you trust and use the pleasure priority (regardless of the results), give yourself an A. Each time you get tense and worry about the outcome (regardless of the results), give yourself an F. What you are creating for yourself is an experiential grading system. If you have a child, what mode does he or she use when producing results – tension and survival or relaxation and creativity?* Encourage your child to view each exam as though it contains two parts. While the teacher will be grading the accuracy of the exam, your child should also be grading himself or herself on the actual experience of taking the exam. When you ask, "How well did you do on the exam?" your child should respond with two grades: the experience and the result.

Another way to experiment with the pleasure priority mode is to have fun and play to lose. I discovered the power of playing to lose several years ago when a girlfriend's father challenged me to a game of tennis. He was a really competitive and aggressive guy who hated to lose. He also would not take no for an answer. I knew my life would be a lot easier with him if I accepted the challenge and purposely lost. I also knew that if he smelled my scheme, he'd go nuts. So I adopted the strategy of staying really loose; I had an enormous amount of fun and rarely remembered the score. The result was that I didn't make enough mistakes. I unfortunately won.

As you begin to perform in more pressurized surroundings, your challenge will be to continue choosing the pleasure priority over a precision priority. How you sell the product or service (your physical, emotional and faithing state) must be more important than the outcome. How you swing the golf club or racquet must take precedence over the results. The present experiential payoff must be valued more than a future payoff. At times this challenging discipline will seem impossible to achieve, so please have patience. There will also be moments when you will be convinced that I am out of my mind. Regardless of your frustration, lack of progress, or anger toward me, I urge you to keep recommitting to the *pleasure priority path* even if it is just for a few seconds a day. The more you can choose an embracing mode

* If your child is producing from any fear or terror look to see if your home environment is unintentionally causing it. Your child needs to feel unconditionally loved each and every time he or she takes an exam (all the way through medical school).

over a bracing one, the more insights and mini-breakthroughs
you eventually will experience in every area of your life. The stories that follow will help to illustrate the power of the pleasure
priority mode.

◆JOHNNY KNAPSACK◆

Johnny Knapsack grew up in a small Midwestern town. He was a
tall, lanky lad with long, skinny legs. He got his nickname because
every day he'd walk to and from school carrying a load of text-
books in his knapsack. One day, on his way home from school, an
upperclassman named Chuck challenged him to a race. Before
he could refuse, the race was on. Johnny had no expectations of
winning, however, because Chuck was the fastest man on the
high school basketball team. You can imagine Johnny's amazement when he beat Chuck to the soda shop.

Word soon spread about his accomplishment, and from that
day forward, life was never quite the same for Johnny. Every day
after school, someone else would challenge him, and every day
without fail Johnny would win. He began to enter regional races
and would walk away with the trophy. After winning the state
championship, a group of neighbors raised some money to cover
his expenses for the Olympic trials.

Once at the trials, Johnny carried on his tradition of winning.
He did so well that he qualified for the final heat. The first four
runners to cross the finish line would qualify for the U.S. Olympic
team. Even though there were seven other men running in the
race, he felt extremely confident that he would be one of the top
four finishers. Although it was a very close and thrilling race,
Johnny came in fifth. Needless to say, he was devastated.

With tears streaming down his face, he began to leave the
field. Suddenly, one of the American coaches ran over to him
and said, "You know, you really should have won that race."
"What are you talking about?" replied Johnny. "I came in fifth.
How in the world could I have won the race?" The coach replied,
"It was a very close race. The difference between the first- and
fifth-place positions was only a fraction of a second. All you had to

do was to take that heavy knapsack off your back and you would have won. Didn't anyone ever tell you to take that stupid thing off your back?"

"Everyone kept telling me to take it off," Johnny replied. "But I always kept winning. I was just following my father's advice – never change a winning game and always change a losing one."

The coach responded, "Johnny, you are so fast and gifted that you have been winning *in spite of* the knapsack, not because of it. Your self-imposed handicap finally caught up with you in this national event."

When Johnny arrived home, he kept thinking about what the coach had said. He decided to experiment by running the next race with one less book on his back. To his amazement, he won the race in record time. In each subsequent race, he kept lightening his load by taking an additional book out. Finally, he was running and winning with an empty knapsack and then without the knapsack at all. He had learned his lesson.

Perhaps there is a little bit of Johnny Knapsack in all of us. Many of us have become successful in spite of our limiting habits, not because of them. We ignorantly drag extra baggage around (tension, abusive substances, perfectionism, or a comfortable yet limiting habit), thinking that these extraneous patterns are actually helping us to succeed.

Every now and then, use The 15 Second Principle to stop, look, and listen. Discover which elements are absolutely necessary for your performing technique and which are unintentional encumbrances. Determine if you can execute the same action or complete the same assignment with more relaxation, energy, focus, and faith. By becoming aware of your restrictive habits and by slowly freeing yourself from these self-imposed handicaps, you will be able to have more fun and freedom as you tap into more of your full potential.

THE ELIXIR OF PERFORMING

A million-dollar cure-all for most performing ills is this: Regardless of how brilliantly or how poorly you are performing, always be in the process of doing *less*. This advice can be applied to every area of our lives (including sports, sales, performing arts, dating, and public speaking). This cure-all "tonic" can also be described as the paradox of performing. In order to remain in flow or regain your performing balance and momentum, you must be willing to back off and do less. This would include changing your focus, releasing tension, freeing yourself from limiting perceptions, slowing things down, and being more efficient by refining your actions. If you are a demanding, compulsive, and/or competitive person (like many of us), this paradoxical concept will be extremely challenging for you. In a sense, to perform even better, you will have to risk performing worse. To accomplish this, you will have to back off, do less, and add an enormous amount of trust to your performing repertoire.

When we were young we encountered the elixir of performing when we wanted to learn how to whistle. Whenever we would place too much tension in our lips, create too large a hole with our mouth, or thrust too much air through the opening, nothing would happen. The harder we worked and the more we attempted to do, the worse our results. It was only by doing less, trusting more, and finding the right blend of air and aperture that we were able to create a sound, a note, and then a song. A similar reality occurs in every aspect of our lives. Less is more. Let's explore some practical areas where we can immediately apply this amazingly simple yet useful approach to excellence.

The Elixir of Sports

Regardless of how wonderful or terrible your last swing or stroke was, try this: On the very next one, *do less*. This will usually entail relaxing your muscles and releasing any residual tension in your fingers, arms, shoulders, jaw, neck, and eyes.

After a Great Shot

Whenever we successfully execute a fluid and relaxed stroke, we have a tendency to think, "If that was a powerful shot when I did nothing, wait until the next one when I do a little *something*." The results more often than not are disastrous. After a wonderfully effortless shot, the trick is to dare to do even less on the very next one. This "lessness" discipline will counterbalance the "more-ness" tendency of our "fixer" self (the one who is just itching to do *more* each time you contact the ball). The result will usually be another accurate, pleasurable, and fluid swing.

After a Terrible Shot

Whenever a swing or stroke is not working well, our first instinct is to do more in order to fix it. Rather than fixing it with relaxation, finesse, and additional trust, we often use tension, pressure, and muscle (in the fingers, arm, shoulder, jaw, and neck) to aggressively force a correction. The result is usually a swing that keeps deteriorating, a drawer that remains stuck, or a key that still doesn't turn in a lock.

When a swing is not working, you must be willing to back off and do less. Once again, this is due to your internal fixer, who wants to try harder, to correct things. Try instead, to relax and slow things down. Oftentimes, a lessness adjustment will get you back on track. Think of the club, racquet, bat, etc., as your brilliant and powerful partner. When you are off, *trust* and let it do more of the work.

This lessness principle will also serve you when you want to produce strokes and swings with more power. Buckminster Fuller's "dymaxion" approach to life can help us here. This brilliant visionary of the 1930s coined the word *dymaxion*, which means getting the maximum gain from the minimum energy input. When we can trust more and do less, especially in the fingers and arms, our swinging instrument will automatically do more. Our dymaxion swinging mission is to have our hands, arms, and shoulders feel more like loose conduits channeling the power, rather than an energy source creating it. Bruce Lee said it best when he stated, "The less effort, the faster and more powerful you will be."

In addition, your objective is to feel the production of the stroke, rather than to see the results of it. By experiencing the pleasurable creation, you will encourage yourself to live more in present time. This sensate approach will encourage your head to remain still until after the moment of contact with the ball. This is because the more pleasurable the experience of the swing, the less of a burning desire you will have to see the results. This, in turn, will add more faith and precision to each shot.

The Elixir of the Performing Arts

This principle can also be applied to the performing arts. Through our desire to be loved, appreciated, and approved of, we will tend to do too much during a performance. Fear of being dismissable will also cause us to push and do too much. (In acting, they call this behavior "chewing up the scenery.") Once again, the challenge of the salesperson, public speaker, first-dater, teacher, singer, painter, or musician is to use the subtle skills of trust and lessness.

This is especially true when things are not working well onstage. In such cases, back off and do less. Do not act like a panicking bull in a china shop by using tension and anxiety to bail out of a situation. Instead, go in the opposite direction. Relax, slow down, and breathe. Center yourself by checking out each one of your senses. Are you really hearing, seeing, touching, tasting, and smelling? Are you relaxed enough to be affected by the feedback your senses are picking up? The purpose of these sensory checks is to reconnect you to your environment and help you to live more in present time. This, in turn, will allow you to do your best work. The pilot who can stay cool while in a tailspin, not panic, and remain in present time is much more likely to find the correct action to pull the plane out of its nosedive.

Your goal is to become more aware of your current performing habits. This awareness will make it less likely that you will automatically rush in and use old and obsolete habits when facing a challenge. Your objective is to be free to choose a different approach when seeking excellence. Apply The 15 Second

Principle by stopping your rote behavior and by substituting a lessness behavior. Regardless of how well or poorly you are currently performing, keep refining and trusting the elixir of performing. What you are really seeking is an effortless and economical technique that will serve you well in most situations and environments. By going in this lessness direction and producing from openness, faith, and grace, you will start developing a powerful technique that will serve you in every area of your life.

SYDNEY'S PERFECTION

When I was growing up in New York, I studied flute for many years with a man named Sydney. Everything about him was correct and precise. His posture, speech, suits, and manicured fingernails all told the story of perfection. Every week, I knew that I had better be prepared. I also prayed that my tone would be clear and that I wouldn't make too many mistakes. While his bark was much worse than his bite, whenever I saw Sydney, I was instantly reminded that music was an exact and serious craft.

Sydney was also one of the best flutists around. He recorded solo flute albums, taught other professionals, and was president of a professional musicians' club. All of this was extremely impressive, but there was one thing about Sydney that I never quite understood. If he was such a great musician, why wasn't he playing regularly with a major symphony orchestra?

This question remained unanswered for many years. Then one day in Los Angeles I happened to walk into a music repair shop. Before long, I found myself talking with an older gentleman who was repairing an ancient clarinet. The conversation quickly shifted into talk of legendary New York musicians. When I brought up Sydney's name, the man was extremely impressed that I had studied with "the great one." At this point, I decided to seek a response to my unanswered question. "If Sydney was so amazing, why wasn't he playing with the New York Philharmonic?"

After hearing the question, the man looked up and, with a sad and humorous expression on his face, he said, "Don't you know about Sydney?"

"No," I answered.

"Well, Sydney got nervous."

"What?" I said.

"Sure, Sydney was the best, but he could get very nervous. Every time Toscanini would call, he'd get white."

At that moment, a large missing piece seemed to fall into place. Sydney's problem was that the perfection he demanded in his students, he also demanded in himself. Perhaps his obsession with precision was the very thing that caused him to feel so nervous. If he hadn't put such a negative value on mistakes and included them in his universe, perhaps he would have enjoyed the performing process more.

From this insight into Sydney, I learned a great lesson regarding professionalism and precision. Our main goal should be to prepare and practice correctly and then to go out and have a relaxed, trusting, and self-expressive time performing. Demanding perfection puts too much of a strain on our system. Ironically, the fear of a mistake and our inability to make room for a possible error are the very things that encourage the mistake to occur. Dwelling on perfection or resisting imperfection will also dilute the amount of trust and passion we can generate in our performance.

The way out of this dilemma is to choose a performing world called self-expression. In this realm, include *all* possibilities (both perfection and imperfection). You are not embracing the mistakes but neither are you resisting or dreading them. Instead, you are including them in the possible performing mix. By embracing a broad spectrum of all the possibilities, you will give yourself more freedom and create a safer environment within which to perform. This will enhance your chances of tapping into an optimum performing state on a more regular basis. Jeanne Baxtresser, principal flute of the New York Philharmonic, says it best in the following quote (from *Flute Talk* magazine):

> *During an audition there should be a sense of spontaneity. It is a human experience to play music. To expect to play a note-perfect audition is unreasonable. I know in my three auditions I did a lot of playing at a high level, and even*

*though I made some mistakes, the music came through
because I was concentrating on sound, musicality, communicating emotion, and technical proficiency. Most players
forget the first three aspects and simply regard the process
of learning excerpts as an Olympic event for speed and
fingers. The music is forgiving: once the notes and rhythm
are secure, players should concentrate on communicating
the essence of the music. It doesn't matter if a note is bob-
bled along the way.*

Whenever you become too results-oriented, apply The 15 Second
Principle. Stop, slow down, and readjust your focus. Your mission
is to shift back into a pleasure-priority mode by executing specific
sensory actions. (We will address these specific actions in "Masters
of 'Relaxion'" on page 000.) This readjustment toward relaxation,
trust, faith, and passion and away from a perfect outcome will
create a safer and more nurturing environment within which to
perform.

*As a performer, for instance, I am interested in pursuing
excellence, but that doesn't mean I always achieve it. I hit
and miss all the time, including in these shows . . . but I
think one of the things that is important in life is to learn
to accept your imperfections, which is something that I
couldn't understand for years.*

—*Barbra Streisand*

BIG BOB'S BREAKTHROUGH

Many years ago, I had a tennis student named Bob. He was six-
foot-three and must have weighed in at three hundred pounds.
He was in his early thirties and appeared to have more baby fat
than muscle tone. As a bookkeeper for an electronics company,
he spent most of his days seated behind a huge desk. Without a
doubt, Bob was the most difficult student I had ever had. I could

never get him to improve. Regardless of what I'd say or what images I used, he'd keep trying to kill each ball with tension and aggression. While he kept showing up for lessons (something I never quite understood), he appeared to be extremely limited in his talent, technique, and capacity to learn.

During a typical lesson he could hit a dozen balls over the fence. Several times I even suggested (begged) that he take up racquetball. I thought the walls of the racquetball court would allow him to keep the ball in play as he let out his power and aggression. He always rejected my idea by responding, "But I love tennis." I could never figure out what he loved about tennis other than the joy of losing my tennis balls.

Before his next lesson, I made an agreement with myself. Either Bob was going to have a breakthrough or I was going to stop teaching him. Perhaps another instructor would have more success reaching him. The first part of the lesson was as frustrating as all the others. He was still attempting to destroy every ball that I hit to him. Out of pure frustration, I requested that we have a meeting at the net. I had no idea what I was going to say to him, but I knew I needed a break.

Approaching the net, I thought of a question. "Bob," I said, "while growing up, did you ever play other sports?" I was sure his answer would be a big *no*.

Instead, he responded, "Just golf."

"You played golf?" I said.

"Yeah, I played it through my senior year of college. In fact, I was runner-up in my state's high school golf championships."

I couldn't believe my ears. "Okay," I said. "Make believe that the tennis ball is a golf ball, and that the racquet is a golf club. Now go back to the baseline and hit the 'golf ball' after it bounces on your side."

Miraculously, Bob began transforming himself into a much more graceful player. His hands, arms, and shoulders became relaxed and trusting. His strokes slowly but surely became loose and fluid. His ball control also had a drastic improvement. In fact, the change was so instantaneous and dramatic that it looked as though Bob had just received a talent transplant.

Up until that moment, Bob was thinking of tennis as a unique and isolated sport. His body and mind never made the connection between tennis and golf. Once he understood their interrelatedness he was immediately able to shift into his golf production center and produce tennis strokes from there. Once the channels were open, Bob was immediately able to transfer faith, relaxation, fluidity, and soft hand control directly into his tennis game.

Whenever we are learning something new, or feeling that we don't have any talent in a specific discipline, we should apply The 15 Second Principle by stopping and reexamining the situation. Rather than excluding what we have already learned, we want to become masters of inclusion. A dancer could apply her gracefulness, posture, and relaxation to tennis. A computer maven whose hands feel very comfortable on the keyboard could apply this same finger comfort when he holds the shaft of a golf club. A dentist who is learning how to shoot pool could imagine that she is just substituting a metal dental instrument for a larger wooden one.

Whenever you become overwhelmed with something new, stop and apply The 15 Second Principle. Discover the similarities between the new endeavor and what you already have mastered. By figuring out the connecting threads in each discipline, you will become a master of interrelatedness. This will enable you to begin most new disciplines further up the proficiency ladder. It will also remind you that the only true beginner is a one-day-old infant.

The Process Is the Message

*People say that what we're all seeking is a meaning for life.
I don't think that's what we're really seeking. I think that what
we're seeking is an experience of being alive, so that our life
experiences on the purely physical plane will have resonances
within our innermost being and reality, so that we actually
feel the rapture of being alive.*

—*Joseph Campbell*

Many years ago, I had the pleasure of meeting James Coburn at a party. He was in Manhattan rehearsing a six-hour miniseries for CBS. Seeing as he was starring in the miniseries, I thought it strange that he was spending precious time at a party. We began talking about many things, one of which was music. I discovered that he had recently started playing the flute (an instrument that I have played since childhood). Toward the end of the evening, I mentioned to him that I had developed an unusual system for practicing and learning the flute and offered to share it with him. I was delighted when he accepted my offer.

Two days later, at ten in the morning, I found myself entering the lobby of the legendary Drake Hotel. The elevator operator took me up to the tenth floor and pointed out the room to me. When Mr. Coburn opened the door, he was wearing a beautiful bathrobe. He looked well rested and relaxed. I was intrigued by his calm and mellow demeanor. After giving me a warm hello, he walked to the phone, dialed some digits, and said, "This is Mr. Coburn. We're ready." *Ready for what?* I thought. A few minutes later, breakfast for two was wheeled into his room. *Now this isn't your ordinary flute lesson,* I thought. As we were eating our melons, I noticed his script for the miniseries sitting on a table. It was at least three inches thick and looked more like the Manhattan phone directory. *God, that's a lot of lines to memorize,* I thought. *How does he have time to take a flute lesson? How come he's so relaxed? The way he's behaving, you'd swear he had just finished the movie. Isn't he supposed to be anxious and uptight right now?*

After a leisurely breakfast, we proceeded to have an hour-and-a-half lesson. The session went so well that he asked whether I could return two days later.

Upon my return to his room, the same scenario occurred. I appeared at ten o'clock, and a few minutes later breakfast was wheeled in. The script looked as thick as ever, and James was just as relaxed. This time, however, I was comfortable enough to ask him some questions about his calm state. I wanted to know how he could be so at ease with so much riding on his performance. Also, I wanted to know why he took time for flute lessons when he could have been working on his part. His answers really turned my head around.

What I learned was that James Coburn approaches the entire craft of acting as a *process*. His goal is to have an enlivening and enriching experience throughout the entire performing schedule. What he discovered after years of trial and error was that if he enjoys the rehearsal process more, his performance is usually better. His creativity and spontaneity get stifled whenever he attempts to close himself off from the outside world. His challenge is always to design a nurturing and enjoyable day for himself rather than a tense and serious one. When he is successful, unexpected insights and experiences occur that ultimately help his performance.

From reading the script to working on his character, from memorizing the lines to rehearsing, from costume fitting to shooting and reshooting a scene, his mission is the same: to enjoy and value each and every step along the way. The first day of rehearsal was just as important to him as the last day of shooting. Each phase of the acting process was valued the same.

It was also interesting to hear that he doesn't consider a star-studded premiere to be an important part of his process. His true excitement and challenge actually ends once his last scene is shot. In fact, he would much prefer to be working on a new project than to be attending one of those gala events at a movie theater.

What turns him on more than viewing the movie is making the movie. He believes that if one's main motivation is to see oneself up on the big screen, then acting is never going to be a truly fulfilling experience. That's because the actor will be giving up many months of his or her life for just two hours of ego fulfillment at the premiere. He believes that's not a very healthy trade-off.

James also tries to control only those things that are within his power. In other words, the things he can't control – the editing, the final cut, the reviewers' taste or the public's opinion – he tries not to worry about. He focuses his attention on his performance and on the experience of making a movie.

*   *   *

If you ever hope to reach your full potential, you must work at your chosen field for a long time. This is a reality that we all must live with. The person who can create an enjoyable journey (one that nurtures and inspires) will never be a victim of his or her own success. This prescription is also very valuable in any competitive endeavor (sports or business, for instance). Your goal should be to enjoy the process of competition. Be as loose when it counts as when it doesn't. In addition, don't use fear of failure as a motivator nor tension as your technique. If you do, you will experience exhaustion and achieve hollow victories.

Bruce Jenner, the gold medal decathlon winner, says it best when he talks about his pursuit of the Olympic gold: "It's the process. The fun part is the journey." It's interesting to note that the word *competition* comes from the Latin word *competere*. Roughly translated, it means "to meet, to seek, to come together, to be influenced by." Nowhere in the Latin translation does it mention superiority, annihilation, or humiliation.

In the sport of tennis, John McEnroe's greatest challenger was Björn Borg. Many of their matches took the world of tennis to new heights. When Björn retired prematurely, John described Borg's surprise departure as his most disappointing moment in tennis. Borg and McEnroe came together to play tennis the way two genius violinists play duets. Apparently, no one could inspire John to reach such brilliant levels as Borg did. Is it any wonder then that McEnroe's passion for tennis and tournament success went downhill after Borg's retirement?

In this chapter, we will continue to emphasize "the process." It's helpful to remember that whenever we make the stakes too high or the results too important, our performance usually suffers. Whenever you sense that you have become too consumed and obsessed by a specific outcome, stop and explore other channels for achieving your goals. This is where The 15 Second Principle can be helpful. By momentarily stopping and detaching from your pursuit, you stand a much better chance of choosing a more pleasurable mode of productivity. This intervening action might be as simple as taking a few deep breaths. Or perhaps what is called for is a different approach, some soothing music, a walk around the block, or a comedic action to break up a serious mood.

The lesson here is to value the process that allows something to be created. The more we can honor the skills of relaxation, energy, focus, and faith, the sooner we will realize that *the process is the message*. When the pressure is on can we still smell a rose, taste the full splendor of a piece of fruit, and feel the warmth of someone's hand? Once we understand the power of living in present time, we will begin to experience more satisfaction, synchronicity, and success regardless of the circumstances.

> *I used to work on parts twenty hours a day, my mind was always working . . . I kind of beat myself up, that if I wasn't digesting this stuff twenty-four hours a day and if I didn't measure up to my own standards, it meant I hadn't worked hard enough . . . A lot of it was working from insecurity and fear. But then I came to realize that . . . you don't have to drive yourself mad.*

> —*Gary Oldman*

◆JOE MONTANA'S COMPETITIVE SECRET◆

Joe Montana is one of the greatest professional football players ever to play the game. He played for the San Francisco 49ers and is considered by many experts to be the best quarterback in the history of football. The following is a story told to me by Bo Eason. Bo was a member of the 49ers and played the free safety position. He is currently a professional actor living in Los Angeles.

Super Bowl XXIII was played in Miami in 1989. The San Francisco 49ers were playing the Cincinnati Bengals. Very late in the fourth quarter Cincinnati broke a tie by scoring a field goal. The score was now 16–13. Cincinnati kicked off, and San Francisco took possession of the ball on their own eight-yard line. To achieve victory, San Francisco would have to travel ninety-two yards and score a touchdown in three minutes and ten seconds.

Before play began, a television commercial time-out was called. To take advantage of this extra time-out, the 49ers went into their own end zone for a huddle. The energy in the huddle was quite charged, nervous, and frenetic. Everyone was trying to inspire everyone else. Suddenly, the players realized that Joe Montana, their team captain and brilliant quarterback, was missing. They all looked up and discovered that Joe was about ten feet away. He was looking directly into the stands and appeared to be quite focused and fascinated.

The guys yelled for Joe to get back into the huddle. After all, they had to get ready for the next play. Joe, however, had something quite different on his mind. "Hey, guys. Hey, guys," he yelled. "You've got to come over here right now and take a look at this." Because he was their inspirational leader and seemed very determined to share his discovery, his teammates rushed to Joe's side. Once they joined him, Joe began pointing into a specific section of the stands. "Look, guys, over there. Look who's sitting right over there. Look. I can't believe it! It's John Candy. Can you believe it? John Candy is watching us play ball."

His teammates looked at Joe, their superstar quarterback, in disbelief. While the world was watching Joe Montana, Joe was fascinated by the fact that the actor John Candy was watching them play football. Had their brilliant leader lost his mind? Didn't he know they only had three minutes left to win the Super Bowl?

History goes on to report that after the television time-out, Joe, with the help of Jerry Rice and Roger Craig, took his team downfield and, with almost no time left, threw a successful touchdown pass to John Taylor in the end zone. San Francisco won the Super Bowl (20–16).

After the game, his teammates realized that their response to the remaining three minutes had been much different from Joe's. While they were rushing and frenetically trying to beat the clock, Joe was feeling and reacting as though he had all the time in the world. Montana's perception of the situation seemed to be different from his teammates'. According to Bo Eason, Joe Montana never played like he was in a stressful and serious emergency. Regardless of whether it was a practice, preseason game, or Super Bowl, Joe treated every situation the same. He responded to each scenario with confidence, looseness, patience, and playfulness. He played the same way regardless of whether he was ahead by three touchdowns or behind by three touchdowns. If anything, Joe appeared to become even more relaxed and alive whenever he was losing or placed in tight situations.

Joe is someone who exemplifies the pleasure priority performing mode. To achieve success, he drew upon relaxation and precise actions. He let pleasure and trust fuel his competitive approach to excellence. He did care a great deal about winning, but worry, fear, and tension were not the competitive tools he relied upon. Instead, he always had the courage to let trust, relaxation, and playfulness be the driving forces that directed his amazing career.

◆THE GROWTH PROCESS◆

Man is not the sum of what he has but the totality of what he does not yet have, of what he might have.

—Jean-Paul Sartre

Nature can provide us with a wonderful insight into the learning and growing process. There is a fascinating species of bamboo called *Dendrocalamus gigantius*. After being planted, it does not show any apparent signs of growth for several years. From an underground perspective, however, an enormous amount of activity continually occurs. Before ever beginning its upward ascent, the plant builds a huge network of roots that spreads deep and wide. The anchoring process can take years to weave.

Once the subterranean support system is in place, *Dendrocalamus gigantius* begins its upward journey. During this phase, the plant will grow at an astounding rate of two to three feet a *day*. Scientists report that by sitting very still, you can almost see the shoots grow. Within several weeks the plant will reach a height of approximately 120 feet.

How long did it take for this plant to reach 120 feet? Is the answer four weeks or four years? I believe we must include the total gestation period along with the vertical sprinting period. Just because we can't see results and physically measure them doesn't mean that growth and progress aren't happening.

As creators, we also need to spend more time developing our own subterranean support system. Before manifesting our dreams, we need to create a deep and wide web of training, planning, and experiencing. It's important to realize that materializing our creation is the last in a series of important steps. Skyscraper contractors spend years drawing up blueprints and digging way down into the earth before ever building skyward.

In a culture desiring instant results and immediate satisfaction, perhaps we are building up before digging down.

- How many small businesses fail because people neglect to raise sufficient capital, do enough research, and get adequate training?

- How many books aren't sold because writers rush the creative process? Submitting a book or proposal before it has been well thought out and polished is a sure way to rejection.

• How many actors fail because their motivation for fame is greater than their motivation for building a solid acting technique and developing strong business skills?

As dedicated seekers, we need patience and trust during our own personal gestation periods. Lowell Ganz, screenwriter of such blockbusters as *City Slickers, Splash,* and *Parenthood,* told me that it takes him and his partner, Babaloo Mandel, more time working out the characters, scenes, and plot than it does to create the 120 pages of actual dialogue.

Tim Gallwey, creator of the best-seller *Inner Tennis,* wrote the book in a very short period of time. What's not mentioned is that he studied Eastern thought and meditation for many years before ever writing the book.

It is said that King David's Temple in Jerusalem took ten years to build. The first eight years were spent on drawing the plans and cutting the individual huge stones.

Nature constantly reminds us that there is nothing wrong with being a late bloomer. It will take an avocado tree approximately seven years to begin to bear fruit. Then, it will only produce avocados every other year.

Likewise, another species of bamboo, called *Fargesia dracocephala,* will flower between forty and sixty years after it is planted. It is also helpful to remember that the Grateful Dead were on the music scene for twenty-one years before they had a hit single with "Touch of Grey." It took Bonnie Raitt eighteen years and ten albums before she had a hit with "Something to Talk About." And Michael Jordan, perhaps the greatest basketball player ever to play the game, failed to make his high school varsity team in his sophomore year.

Each person, like each species, is unique unto him- or herself. We have our own maturation timetable, which we must honor. We must give ourselves (and our children) permission to grow and unfold at our own pace. We need to maintain a constant vigilance not to allow any of these *eight pitfalls to performing excellence* prevent us from following our hearts and staying committed to our mission:

1. Comparing our progress with that of our contemporaries

2. Not believing in ourselves enough

3. Feeling it's too late to begin

4. Looking for constant approval

5. Wanting to control the precise outcome of every endeavor

6. Not taking corrective actions

7. Not continuing after we encounter an obstacle

8. Not celebrating our mini-successes along the way

If you ever feel yourself being lured into any one of these eight pitfalls, stop and apply The 15 Second Principle. Your goal is to separate yourself from these addictive and destructive internal conversations. By nipping these inner dialogues in the bud, they will have less power to negate your journey. This will make it less likely that you will demand visible results every minute of every day. Being relentlessly consumed with measurable progress is not the most masterful way to approach your dreams or life. Instead, what is most important is to keep showing up with passion, patience, practice, and planning!

A gentle yet cautionary word is also needed here. Make sure that your "rooting process" also contains integrity. There is a time for contemplation and a time for manifestation. You want to have respect for your own maturation process, but be sure not to let fear, activities, and laziness masquerade as preparation, rejuvenation, and meditation. As Will Rogers advised us, "Even if you're on the right track, you'll get run over if you just sit there."

Eventually, tangible mini-actions must also be taken. Although the tortoise did beat the hare, he won by getting out on the road and walking at his own pace toward his goal. He didn't win by sitting under a tree and sulking about his difficult lot in life – short legs, a thick neck, and a heavy load. At some point, if your phobias, misgivings, and shortcomings refuse to go away, you will have to pick them up, embrace them, and carry them across that primal threshold that separates rumination from creation. When you do, miraculous things will happen.

> *Why should we be in such a desperate haste to succeed and in such desperate enterprises? If man does not keep pace with his companions, perhaps it is because he hears a different drummer. Let him step to the music which he hears, however measured or far away.*

> —*Henry David Thoreau*

◆ESCAPING FROM QUICKSAND◆

Years ago, there were many jungle movies on television. While the plots in these dramas ran thin, you may remember that the quicksand ran thick and deep. There always seemed to be these mysterious puddles of death hidden behind patches of foliage. You never knew who would wind up in these dangerous holes of muck. Would it be the hero or the villain?

Although I haven't seen one of these "masterpieces" in years, I can still remember the nature and theme of the scenes. The bad guys would always struggle to escape, and they would invariably sink. To the viewer it was always apparent that panicking, fighting, and struggling to get out were sure prescriptions for death. If, however, a good guy or gal could relax, surrender, and accept the reality of the moment, he or she always survived. By staying calm and working with the quicksand, the person thought more clearly, took the necessary slow actions, and found salvation.

You can apply this principle to many pressure-filled scenarios. Whenever you find yourself in a situation you would rather not be in, don't oppose or fight it the way you would an enemy. Most of the time desperation, tension, and aggression will be the wrong choices. Instead, surrender to the reality of the situation and work soft, not hard. By surrendering to these unwanted and challenging circumstances, you will be able to work with them and not against them. The result will be a more nurturing experience in a stress-filled environment.

Surrendering is an elusive concept to describe and experience. I am not referring to giving up, forfeiting, or conceding. Rather, I am describing something that is just the opposite. Surrendering is an opening and accepting of a situation. The easiest way to understand surrendering is to think back to the time you learned how to float. When developing this skill, what you discovered was that the more tension you used, the faster you would sink; the more fear you felt, the less buoyant you were; the more you tried not to drown, the more you sank; conversely, the more you relaxed and trusted, the more buoyant you became.

This floating and surrendering process can also become a valuable tool in helping you to work well on land. Whenever you find yourself in a quicksand type of situation, first apply The 15 Second Principle. Rather than approaching the problem head-on with tension, fear, seriousness, and aggression, stop and dare to risk by approaching the situation from the opposite end of the spectrum. Tony Danza describes his opposite-end-of-the-spectrum approach in acting, singing, and boxing as "the courage to remain calm." By not getting caught up in the drama of the moment, we are able to be more relaxed and to think more clearly. By residing in the calm eye of the hurricane, rather than in its turbulent periphery, we improve our chances of coming up with better solutions and more appropriate actions.

◈ELVIS'S WALK◈

Before becoming a successful motion picture actor, Billy Drago worked for Elvis Presley during one of his tours. Billy told me about a fascinating process that Elvis would go through just before performing. Hours before the concert, some members of Elvis's staff would arrive at the performing venue and meticulously measure a distance that was *exactly* one thousand yards away from the arena, theater, or hall. Finally, Elvis's large dressing-room trailer would be placed on this distant spot.

A few hours before show time, Elvis would arrive and enter this trailer. From Billy's viewpoint, Elvis rarely appeared ready or able to work. In fact, it appeared that he needed an energy and charisma transfusion. According to Billy, even after Elvis showered and changed into his costume, he was still in a low-energy state.

Elvis would remain in this nonenergized state even after he left his trailer and started on his thousand-yard walk toward the venue. As the walk progressed, however, something incredible always happened. With each step, Elvis would slowly but surely regain his energy, vitality, and focus.

By the time he reached the venue, Elvis would be radiating an enormous amount of energy and charisma. In fact, according to Billy, Elvis's energy field became so radiant and powerful that the audience would miraculously sense his presence before he ever entered the venue. They'd react by going into a clapping and screaming frenzy. This would continue until Elvis entered the venue and finally appeared onstage. The rest is history.

It's important to note that whenever Elvis would begin his walk, he was not trying to cover up his low-energy state. Instead, he was being authentic with his fatigue. He did not pretend that he was ready to perform. Rather, he accepted and began from wherever he was at – a low-energy state. Elvis was congruent with his emotions every step of the way.

Another helpful point is that Elvis became electrified *before* he took the stage. He didn't wait for the audience to energize him. Rather, he took responsibility for energizing himself. Apparently, this process was so successful that the audience felt his presence even before he entered center stage. He accomplished this by walking his way into a potent, positive, and passionate state.

It would be extremely helpful for you to develop your own preparatory process. Before you give a sales presentation or speech, before you compete or audition, before you perform or go on an important date, invent your own personal warm-up approach. When getting creative, remember that if you are in a negative mood or are exhausted, your goal is first to embrace the current state and to be authentic with your feelings. Next, you want to convert that state into a *positive emotional and physical state*.

Elvis did it with his walk. How will you do it? Some healthy options are jogging, relaxation exercises, swimming, breathing exercises, meditations, a short nap, making or listening to music, and finishing your shower with cold water. What you are seeking is a physical and emotional opening, a positive shift in energy, attitude, relaxation, and emotions.

Use The 15 Second Principle to stop and take stock of your physical and emotional states. Honor where you currently are rather than where you wish you were. The goal is to design a technique that helps you transform a down, low-energy state into an *up, high-energy state*. This approach will allow you to become more vibrant yet calm, powerful yet relaxed. By changing your behavior, you can improve your state, which in turn will enhance the quality of your performance. By treating the preparatory process with as much respect as the actual performance, as Elvis did, you will add another dimension to your mini-action repertoire.

◆ AFTER STATE ◆

It's extremely important to become more aware of how you are feeling during a show, event, or gathering. With this awareness you can begin to take mini-actions to guide you back on track whenever you veer off course. Unfortunately, this instant awareness is not always possible. Many times we get so involved with our performance (speaking at a conference, selling a service, being on a date, competing, or attending a gathering), that we are not aware of what it takes, mentally and physically, to get through the event. Even when a performance or occasion is over, you can still learn a lot about how well you performed by evaluating your current mental and physical condition. With this in mind, let's explore a feeling I refer to as "after state."

After an event or performance, assess your physical and mental condition. Are you exhilarated or exhausted, elated or relieved, empowered or powerless? Are you feeling happy and comfortable or does it feel like you just escaped from the jaws of a lion? Are you feeling fulfilled or are you in desperate need of a compliment? Are you energized or does it feel like you just gave four pints of blood?

In addition, realize that just because you achieved a goal, you may not necessarily have used the energy in your body in the most efficient manner. Sometimes when our survival mechanisms get triggered we call upon tension and terror to get us through the performance. At times, we can even get lucky and "win" using this draining mode of performing. What we need to know is that even though we hit our mark, our body, mind, and soul paid a price.

If after a meeting, party, or conversation, you are feeling drained, angry, or relieved, try to recollect when these negative feelings began. Was it before the event began, or did these feelings emerge during the occasion? Attempt to determine the exact moment this shift in thought, energy, and/or emotion began. This investigatory process will assist you in determining when – and hopefully why – your experience became less than satisfactory. Sometimes an uncomfortable after-state feeling will simply mean that you shouldn't be in the company of toxic, self-indulgent, and abusive people. Conversely, be on the alert when you are feeling ecstatic after a party. Sometimes this type of after state may indicate that you had too much to drink, or that you prematurely fell in love. If it's the love bug, go slowly and remember that what goes way up, fast, usually comes way down, fast.

After any performance or gathering, apply The 15 Second Principle by stopping and analyzing your feelings and emotions. Even if you lost a competition or missed a sale, it's still possible to feel a positive after state. We are not talking about results, we are talking about the type of experience you created for yourself. Remember, the more aware you can become about the quality of your after-state condition, the more skillful you will ultimately become during the performance.

◆ THE KING, MORTY AND THE FLYING CHICKEN ◆

There once was an almighty king who ruled over the land of Chickendom. One day while looking at the national flag flapping in the wind, he thought about giving it a face-lift. To accomplish this, he decided to put the picture of a large flying chicken on it. Because the king was no fool, he called for Morty, the best artist in the land. When Morty arrived, the king told him of his wishes. "I want you to paint the most magnificent chicken flag in the world." The king gave Morty rolls of silk and sent him on his way.

The king waited for weeks, but he never heard back from Morty. Finally, one morning, after a three-hour pedicure, the king called out, "Saddle my horse and bring me one hundred of my best soldiers. I'll make this Morty fellow regret the day he ever accepted this assignment." So off they rode: the king, his hundred soldiers, and Ha Ha, the court jester. After twenty miles of riding, they approached Morty's hut. Inside, they could hear him passionately singing, "I'm gonna live, live, live, until I die." The king barked, "Bring that tone-deaf fool out here and tie him to the nearest tree."

Within seconds Morty, with paintbrushes still in hand, was dragged feet first out of his hut. Naturally, he had stopped singing. "Bring me my golden spears," the king demanded. Morty's posture had never been better, as thick ropes pressed his spine firmly against a huge oak tree. The king raised his spear and shouted, "How dare you take my command so lightly! I told you to paint me the most magnificent chicken flag in all the world and you never delivered the goods. Now, my soldiers will have to deliver their goods. No one deserves to live after making a fool out of the king. Prepare to die."

Suddenly, Ha Ha sprinted up to the king and whispered, "Oh, you all-powerful king, you. I agree that Morty deserves to die. But if you kill him now, you still won't have a flag. Remember, he is still the best artist in the entire kingdom. Why not untie that lazy lump of lizard lard and let him paint the flag? *Then* the boys can use him for target practice." The king began to smile. "Ha Ha," he said, "you stink as a comedian, but as a wise man, you're not bad. Untie the swine and bring out all of his painting supplies. Morty, you've got one hour to paint the best flying chicken in all the land. If you succeed, you'll die quickly; if you fail, be prepared for a slow and painful death."

After weighing his options for a minute, Morty began painting. Within one hour he had completed his task. The king dismounted and walked over to the canvas. Unexpectedly, he began to cry. He turned to Morty and said, "This is the most magnificent flying chicken I've ever seen. You are truly a brilliant artist. Why didn't you paint that weeks ago? If you had, I wouldn't have to kill you now." To answer the king's question, Morty led everyone into his hut and said, "I didn't paint that picture weeks ago because I couldn't." He then opened a huge closet and revealed thousands of paintings of flying chickens all hanging up in neat rows. "It took me all this time to figure out how to paint the right chicken. With or without your prodding, I was finally ready to paint the official chicken flag today." The king, being a reasonable man, embraced Morty, gave him a small golden chicken, and promoted Ha Ha to a serious cabinet position.

The moral of the story is that the "strokes" of an artist, athlete, sales person, public speaker, mechanic, comedian, or musician are all very similar in that each must be practiced. When Morty painted his final chicken flag, the king thought it was the first one he had ever created. Nothing could have been farther from the truth.

Anytime you feel discouraged, exhausted, or overwhelmed, apply The 15 Second Principle by doing one more "brush stroke." Don't let a hopeless mood, lethargy, or fatigue render you powerless to control your own actions. To counterbalance your inertia, perform a self-intervention by taking at least one more small action toward your goal. While the action might feel useless, like a drop in the ocean, do it anyway. This mini-action is your ticket back to commitment and momentum. In closing, let's listen to Ben Hogan, one of the greatest golfers ever to pick up a club, as he describes in his book, *Five Lessons,* one of his most famous golf swings. The swing was created at the Open at Merion and it enabled him to enter a playoff and win the title.

> . . .[T]he view I take of this shot (and others like it) is markedly different from the view most spectators seem to have formed. They are inclined to glamorize the actual shot since it was hit in a pressureful situation. They tend to think of it as something unique in itself, something almost

*inspired, since the shot was just what the occasion called
for. I don't see it that way at all. I didn't hit that shot then
– that late afternoon in Merion. I'd been practicing that
shot since I was twelve years old.*

◆OVERWHELMED? HOW TO GET UNDERWHELMED◆

Being overwhelmed by work, an assignment, or just the mundane
chores of life is a terrible feeling. It brings up debilitating emotions of hopelessness and impending doom. To assist you whenever these feelings arise, it's helpful to look at the entire situation
from a different perspective. To do this you need to separate the
reality of the situation from the emotion of it. Is the task really
impossible or does it just feel that way? Are these impossible feelings similar to any you had as a child? Although emotionally you
might feel that the situation is impossible (such as clean-ing the
house alone after a huge party), intellectually you know that if you
execute enough actions for enough hours, the job will get done.
Once you can label the origin of these overwhelming feelings as
being more psychological than physical, you can view the entire
situation from a more powerful and manageable perspective.

The next step is to view the challenging scenario as an *emotional logjam*. Logjams occur not because there are too many trees but
because all of the trees are simultaneously trying to squeeze
through a narrow opening. To deal with this type of a jam you
have to create some space by moving a few logs away from the
narrow opening and then allowing them to go through one by
one. Eventually, all the logs will pass through.

All emotional logjams occur for the same reason. We *simultaneously experience* our undone tasks as one looming and awesome
entity. We then feel we have to complete the tasks all at once.
This, in turn, can paralyze us. If you become overwhelmed by an
emotional logjam, do the following:

1. Realize that your challenging dilemma is temporary and not impossible to accomplish.

2. Pick someone you know who could complete this project. Then make believe you are this person by acting like him or her.

3. Accept the fact that you are capable of doing only one action at a time.

4. Pick *one* task, the easiest one, and complete it.

5. Pick a second task and do it.

6. Pick a third task and do it.

Continue with this simple approach until you have completed your entire assignment. By breaking up your overwhelming tasks into less intimidating and more manageable *mini-actions,* you will be better equipped to deal with your emotional logjams whenever they appear in your life.

> *The secret of getting ahead is getting started. The secret of getting started is breaking your complex and overwhelming tasks into small manageable tasks, and then starting on the first one.*
>
> —*Mark Twain*

Creating the Environment for More Ultimate Performances

There are some things which can not be learned easily (quickly) – they are the very simplest things, and because it takes a man's life to know them, the little each man gets is very costly and the only heritage he has to leave.

—*Ernest Hemingway*

Several years ago, I was fortunate enough to see Diana Ross perform at Caesar's Palace in Las Vegas. There I was, in a front-row seat at Circus Maximus, watching one of the greatest entertainers of our time. What I experienced was a passionate and perfect performance. It was also inspiring to feel the love that was constantly being exchanged between Diana Ross and her fans.

Afterward, I was able to go backstage and talk to Diana about her wonderful and flawless show. She was quick to point out that her show was not perfect. In fact, there was a moment in one of her songs when she realized that her focus and concentration were off. That was very surprising to hear because that had not been apparent to me. She said that I probably didn't notice it because she got herself back on track very quickly. Fascinated, I asked her just how she accomplished this feat.

Diana graciously revealed that when she was off, she regained her focus by asking herself a simple question: What is the real purpose for my being on stage? Her instant response was to give and receive love. She immediately realized that the reason she was off was that she had become distracted and had left this giving and receiving mode. Once she realized this, she took specific actions to bring herself back to a more loving state. She selected *one* receptive person at a nearby table and started singing and sending love directly to that person. Once she connected with this person, she expanded her focus by including the entire table. Within a few seconds, she had the entire room back in her command. (When applying this midperformance technique yourself, remember to pick a person who is *already* enjoying your performance, someone who is showing warmth and acceptance. You need an immediate and receptive safe harbor to sail to. Don't look to convert someone who is not having fun. He or she might have had a death in the family, not speak your language, or be the world's worst grouch.)

Diana Ross's statement helped me to look at mastery and performing excellence in a totally new light. Before our conversation, I always assumed that becoming a consummate performer meant that eventually you would achieve perfection. That is, the better you got at performing, the fewer mistakes you would make until you were able to achieve flawless performances. After our conversation, I realized that *an ultimate performance is more about passion and correction than it is about perfection.* The ultimate performer doesn't fear or obsess about being off because she knows how to take specific actions that will enable her to recover.

Morihei Uyeshiba, the founder of aikido, also views excellence in a similar fashion. When asked whether he ever loses his center and balance, he replied, "Yes, all the time, but I regain it so fast that you do not see me lose it."

A professional tightrope walker is someone who also understands the importance of corrections. Her success is always determined by how well she can keep herself balanced as she walks a fine line. By continually making adjustments with her feet, arms, and head, she is able to work in harmony with the laws of gravity. She arrives at her destination because she has become a master of correction, not perfection.

It's fascinating to hear Greg Louganis talk about competitive diving. Greg, an Olympic gold medal champion, is perhaps the greatest diver in the history of the sport. In an interview with George Leonard, he revealed that 90 percent of the time, he was not able to leap off the diving board in a perfect manner. So, for

Greg to have created those gold medal dives, he was constantly in a state of midair correction.

Another name for correction and recovery is The 15 Second Principle. In order to have more mini-breakthroughs in your personal and professional life, you must learn how to convert interruptions and detours into mini-breakthroughs. Whenever you feel you are in a tailspin situation, do the following:

1. Don't take the problem personally. Develop another eye that enables you to detach yourself from the immediacy of the situation. This will enable you to think, act, and feel from a fresher and more objective place. If you were an emergency room doctor trying to save the life of a young boy whose parents are weeping and screaming in the reception room, to do your best work, you can't afford to let their panic and pain overly influence you. To take the most appropriate actions, you would have to remain calm, trusting, and focused. At some point, you would have to become larger than the situation; otherwise, you would become a victim of it.

2. Your goal is to take quick mini-actions that will guide you back into an experiential performing mode. More often than not, what caused you to go off course in the first place is your veering into a *result, approval,* or *control* mode. It is difficult to live and perform in present time when you are totally obsessed with reaching a goal, receiving accolades, and controlling everyone and everything around you.

Regardless of how well we understand our craft, some days are still going to be better than others. It is said that after an incredible Shakespearian performance, Sir Laurence Olivier came backstage in a fury. "What's the matter?" a fellow thespian purportedly asked. "You just received all of those curtain calls. Everyone agrees you were brilliant tonight."

"Thank you, I appreciate the compliment," Olivier is said to have replied, "but why tonight and not every night?"

Our goal must be to strive for new heights while developing corrective skills for when we are veering off course. That's all we can really ask for. The more refined our adjustment actions, the smoother the recovery and the better our results. In this chapter, we will be discussing more specific ways in which to produce a safe and nurturing environment. This, in turn, will help us to tap into more of our potential as we create more satisfaction and success.

◆FACING A CHALLENGE◆

Anthropologists, after studying the survival instincts of primates, have discovered that when groups of apes, chimps, and monkeys are faced with an outside danger, these animals will immediately come together and huddle. Rather than scattering and facing the serious problem alone, they *first* run together and embrace. While embracing and huddling, they do not try to hide the fear that is running rampant through their bodies. Instead, they *reveal an emotional authenticity* by releasing their feelings. After emoting, the primates appear calmer and braver as they confront the impending danger together.

Physicists tell us that even atoms have a built-in need to reach out and to come together. Apparently, atoms have little extensions called va-lences. Valences resemble little arms that reach out and connect with other atoms. In a sense, the valences allow molecules to be formed. If billions of atoms in our body are naturally attracted to each other, we can only imagine what the need for camaraderie is in each human body.

Dr. Robert Maurer, an authority in the field of performance anxiety and a professor of psychology at UCLA, has studied the traits of very successful people. What he discovered was that when the going gets tough for successful people, rather than heading into isolation, they get going toward a coach, advisory team, support group, therapist, or loved one. Somehow, successful people have discovered that it is not wise or healthy to go it alone. They know the larger the crisis and challenge, the more they need to reach out. They understand that only an arrogant fool would make an important decision in a think tank built for one.

The first step in applying the "huddling" technique is to become more aware of what your natural tendency is when the emotion of fear rears its head. Do you seek companionship, or do you attempt to go it alone? If you have a tendency to become the Lone Stoic, or the Resolute Martyr, challenge yourself to take one small mini-action away from isolation and toward a caring person or supportive group. Apply The 15 Second Principle by seeking a safe haven in which to be authentic with your feelings. The challenge is always to be honest about your emotions without milking them to death.

Another interesting discovery Dr. Maurer has made about successful people is that when they "huddle," they do *not* talk in terms of confidence and courage. Rather, they express themselves in terms of fear and of being afraid. This is a fascinating discovery because you would think that highly successful people would not choose to dwell in the language of fear. You'd imagine that as a group they'd be more fearless or in denial of their fear. It turns out that just the opposite is true. In a sense, successful people view fear as a natural human emotion that needs to be felt, expressed, and released. They are not embarrassed or apologetic about having the emotion. Instead of running away from it, they talk about it and embrace it. This approach tends to dissipate the fear. (Often, they discover that the fear is being triggered by early childhood memories and associations.)

After hearing about these discoveries, one has to wonder whether an incapacity to relate to fear can cause excessive stress. Perhaps people who are afraid to face their fear, who deny it, or who fight it, are the ones who are stressing out the most. If this is true, then we need to develop a healthier relationship with fear. What's most important is the realization that fear has nothing to do with weakness or failure. Rather, fear is a wonderful indicator that a given thing is important to you. Otherwise, why would it trigger such a powerful survival mechanism?

Dr. Maurer has a simple yet powerful "fear exercise" that can transform your relationship with this emotion. It's called the "I'm Scared of _____ Exercise." It can be done with a partner, a group, or alone. If done daily, it can free you from a lot of debilitating emotions. It works very simply: Keep repeating the sentence and filling in the blank with whatever feelings come up for you. The following is a sample exercise.

1. I'm scared of *failure*.

2. I'm scared of *success*.

3. I'm scared of *new things*.

4. I'm scared of *losing control*.

5. I'm scared of *being alone*.

6. I'm scared of *dark places*.

7. I'm scared of *responsibility*.

8. I'm scared of *growing up*.

9. I'm scared of *being broke and homeless*.

10. I'm scared of *commitment*.

11. I'm scared of *getting out of bed*.

12. I'm scared of *growing old*.

13. I'm scared of *myself*.

14. I'm scared of *disappointing my parents*.

Whatever comes to mind, say it. What's most important is *not* to censor or put a value judgment on anything you say or feel. The longer you stay with this exercise, the better.* At some point the

* If you have deep-seated fears and serious phobias, be careful with this exercise. If you become more fearful and anxious as you fill in the blanks, stop this exercise immediately. This exercise was designed to lighten your load, not to make it worse.

fear will usually stop being so serious and debilitating and instead will become less significant, perhaps even humorous. You will realize that if you are afraid of so many things (and many of us are), perhaps the fear is just a protective illusion of our minds. In this context, a great definition of FEAR is False Evidence Appearing Real.

There are basically two types of fear. First, there is real, life-threatening fear. If a lion or street gang were chasing you, you would be experiencing this type of real fear. Second, there is personal or perceived fear. This would include most types of performance anxiety – stage fright, fear of failing an exam, fear of making a fool out of yourself. I'd like you to entertain the possibility that personal fear doesn't start off as fear at all – that instead, it initially is actually a series of strong and uncomfortable body sensations, such as butterflies in the stomach, excessive sweating, a quickening of the breath, headaches, nausea, etc. While these are very unpleasant feelings, none of them is fear.

What if fear is created by our panicking and fighting these uncomfortable body sensations? What if it is our resistance to these sensations – our fear of these feelings – that throws kerosene onto a small fire? Let's remember that what we resist, persists. The way out of this dilemma is to allow the discomfort to enter and roam around our bodies. By making room for it, the discomfort will be less likely to blossom into debilitating fear. (Remember "The Inclusion Factor" on page 29 and see also "The Door Process" on page 143.)

If and when the discomfort grows into fear, don't fight or hide from it. Instead, do as singer Al Jarreau suggests and get accustomed to the fear. He believes that adrenaline provides an abundance of energy that we can use to perform. The challenge, he told me, is to "channel the energy." Several years ago, on "Larry King Live," Frank Sinatra revealed that whenever he performed onstage, he would always get nervous for the first four seconds. Perhaps by the fifth second, Sinatra had already channeled this burst of extra adrenaline into passion and excitement.

Keep remembering that many of our worries come from the hobgoblins in our mind, which create their own perceptions, realities, and recommendations. The more you can change your patterns, by reaching out to others and by transforming your relationship with your fear, the more masterful you will become in every area of your life.

When you share fear with someone you love and/or respect,
the fear will go away.

—Mike Krzyzewski,
Duke University's basketball coach

◈SILENCE IN GOLDEN◈

Recently I was having lunch with a group of people at UCLA, one of whom was named Kendall. He had a very calm and peaceful demeanor. He was the kind of person I instantly liked and felt comfortable with. Kendall turned out to be a former divinity student. He had just left his church's compound after living on the grounds for eight years. I asked him what his most helpful learning experience was while he was living in this monk-type atmosphere. He smiled and told the following story.

One of Kendall's duties as a divinity student was to accompany ministers as they performed their daily tasks and rituals. Sometimes he would accompany them to counseling sessions where they would meet with troubled members of the congregation. Of the twelve ministers who lived in the compound, two of them interested Kendall the most.

One was Brother John. John was the brightest and most scholarly minister. He had a voracious appetite for reading and assimilating information. He was very perceptive, astute, and witty. Brother John was also a most compelling and vibrant orator. He could command the attention of an entire auditorium. At the pulpit, no one compared to him.

The second minister was Brother Sebastian. He was the oldest and most rotund minister. In his few spare hours a week, he loved to tend to the gardens. Unlike Brother John, he was an extremely boring lecturer. While Brother Sebastian had a very warm personality, his lectures from the pulpit could be described as tedious and uninspiring.

Because he was fascinated by the field of psychology, Kendall once asked Brother John how he approached the process of counseling. Was there a principle or philosophy that he followed when he conducted his sessions? Brother John responded that in order to counsel people, you needed to be sure to create some emotional distance. He told Kendall that to do your best work and give your best advice, you had to maintain your objectivity. If you got too involved, you would lose your clarity and point of view. Each and every time Kendall witnessed John dispensing his verbal prescriptions, he was impressed by Brother John's insight and keen advice.

Kendall held Brother John in great respect, but he also noticed an interesting pattern. Although Brother John's advice was of the highest order, very few people seemed to be benefiting from it. Every week, the same divinity students would come back to him with the same problems and questions. Brother John seemed quite concerned and discouraged that so few students were benefiting from his wisdom.

At the same time, Kendall observed that students seeking Brother Sebastian's advice were experiencing better results. Through his counseling sessions, people appeared to be getting on with their lives with less pain and struggle. Their recurring problems seemed to be less persistent and emotionally debilitating.

Kendall posed the same question to Brother Sebastian regarding his counseling technique. The meek Brother Sebastian admitted that he had no strict philosophy or system. He also became a little embarrassed when he admitted that he rarely if ever offered specific advice. "What do you do then?" asked Kendall. "I don't know," Brother Sebastian said. "I guess I just listen and pray. The deeper I listen, the more vulnerable I become. The more vulnerable I become, the more I feel like my student. I become an empathetic conduit. Their pain temporarily becomes my pain. Their suffering temporarily becomes my suffering. Their tears become my tears. Most of the time I listen in silence with my heart. After this merging of emotions, I make sure to release any painful or negative feelings that may still be lingering."

I listen in silence with my heart. What Brother Sebastian was referring to was the power of compassion, where the sharer and the listener merge into the same space. Most of us have the desire to help people and to fix their problems. Sometimes this desire gets the best of us as we prematurely stop the healing process by offering advice too quickly. Rather than allowing more time to experience what it is like, emotionally, to walk in their shoes, we want to solve their problem by immediately offering a new and better pair of shoes. Another interesting aspect to this came up when, on separate occasions, I had the pleasure of speaking to Jack Lemmon and Danny Glover about the performing arts. Each of them, when I asked what the most important element of his acting technique was, responded with the word "listening."

The 15 Second Principle can be very valuable in assisting you to listen. Whenever someone is sharing emotions, revealing a problem, or having a heated debate with you, resist the automatic temptation to interrupt and quickly dispense your helpful wisdom. Instead, get more involved and connected by remaining silent or asking an important question. Rather than rushing to solve the problem or win the argument, become more curious and empathetic. Slow down, settle in, and attempt truly to be with that person. Rather than stealing the spotlight or grabbing the microphone by becoming the wise advisor, let the person remain on center stage by continuing to share his or her emotions. If you must speak, use compassionate phrases, such as "I understand," "It seems like you are feeling [thus]," "I appreciate what you're going through." Above all, try to refrain from giving advice or being judgmental.

What most people desire is to be emotionally heard. We can accomplish this "listening" with less analysis, opinions, and chatter circulating in our minds. Dr. James Gottfurcht, a renowned psychologist in the field of empathy and psychology of money, said it best in one of his UCLA lectures: "True listening is a uniquely powerful way both to connect with and to heal people. To offer this gift, we must temporarily surrender our ego, i.e., our preoccupation with ourselves, our judgments and thoughts of how to 'fix' others. Then we can devote ourselves to listening with every cell of our body."

If each of us has the capacity to heal others simply in the way we listen, then we should all be in the endless process of refining our listening skills. Let's remember that *it is the interested person, rather than the interesting one, who is loved and appreciated the most.*

WHY ARE MOST FAMOUS CHEFS MEN?

Without this playing with fantasy no creative work has ever yet come to birth. The debt we owe to the play of imagination is incalculable.

—*C. G. Jung*

Throughout the world, many more women cook than men. If this is the case, why do more men pursue "chefdom," and why are most of the famous chefs still men? Perhaps the answer lies in a man's background. Consider this *possible* scenario:

1. When boys are growing up, there is usually less pressure put on them to learn how to cook. Their families do not brainwash them into thinking that to be a valuable and loved man, they will need to master culinary skills. With less pressure comes more freedom and passion.

2. Boys will hang out in the kitchen and cook only if they are enjoying themselves. They will mix food much the same way they would mix chemicals in a chemistry set. Because boys have less reverence for the "old family recipe," they feel freer to experiment with new variations on familiar, respected themes. Because they bring less awe to the cooking process, they are better equipped to treat it more as a creative art form.

3. As the family is not expecting anything great to appear on the table, when a boy presents something halfway edible, he will be highly praised. This, in turn, will instill more confidence in him.

If you want to experiment with this freedom concept, place a sign in the entryway of the kitchen that reads, THE MISTAKE CENTER. As this gives every chef in the family more freedom to fail, see how much more creativity and curiosity develops.

It's interesting to note that when a musician is playing well and is in a groove, he is described as "cooking." In this state, the musician is simultaneously pleasing himself, his fellow musicians, and the audience. Perhaps there's an important lesson here. By "cooking" more and worrying less, we stand a better chance of having more fun in every endeavor of our lives.

Whenever you find yourself worrying too much about results and not focusing enough on the experience you are currently creating for yourself, stop and apply The 15 Second Principle. Your goal is to shift a result-oriented process into a more creative and nurturing one. The secret is to care less while not being careless. By lowering the stakes, you will create a safer and freer environment for yourself and others. By not trying to prove something, get recognition, or make a monumental difference on the planet, you will unleash an enormous amount of playfulness and creativity. This alone will increase the chances of producing exceptional results.

ARE YOU LIVING IN A SOAP OPERA?

What if you found out that the family you were born into was actually a TV soap opera family and that you were an actor or actress playing a character on the show? What if all your current weaknesses and fears (as well as your strengths) belonged to your soap opera character? What if your doubts, moods, insecurities, anger, addictions and unsupportive relationships were those of your character? What if you also found out that you had the freedom to play other parts in other plays?

If you are excited about this as even a remote possibility, then you will need to know how to expand your acting repertoire. This way you can experience more pleasure and less pain as you tap into more of your potential. The first step is to identify your soap opera character. For all practical purposes assume your soap opera character is all of you. This will include everything about you: your intellect, personality, sarcasm, emotions, likes, dislikes, fears, disciplines, addictions, skills, all the great and terrible aspects – everything. Even the voice inside your head who is currently agreeing or disagreeing with this concept is also your soap opera character.

It doesn't matter much where this character came from or how it got molded and programmed into "you." It might be due to your family environment.* Or it might be your unique DNA configuration. Or you might have brought it with you from a former life (assuming you believe in reincarnation). All of this is irrelevant. What does matter is that you keep identifying more and more specific aspects of your soap opera character.

Next, your goal is to *include,* rather than reject, every nuance of this character. This embracing aspect will be very challenging, yet extremely important. The more you can make room for all of your undesirable feelings and traits, the more you will experience that you are greater than the sum of all these characteristics. Your goal is to use the characteristics of your current soap opera character when they are appropriate, and to choose more dynamic characteristics from other soap opera characters when they are more appropriate. To make things more concrete, here are a few specific examples of what I am talking about:

1. If you suffer from low self-esteem, perhaps this is *your character's* poor self-identity and not yours. Once you understand this and embrace your low-self-esteem character, you will be freer to explore a variety of other traits as well. It is interesting to note that most people with superiority complexes develop this superior attitude trait in order to cover up their low self-esteem. After all, if they really felt great about themselves, they wouldn't have a need to generate a superior demeanor.

2. If you are spending your life trying to "find yourself" and are never successful, perhaps this is your soap opera character's mission and not yours. What if your character has been pre-programmed and is destined *never* to find him- or herself?

---

* My older sister Judy spoke and read at a very young age, whereas my character, knowing these areas were already taken, got a lot of mileage and attention by choosing stammering and dyslexia as characteristics.

Once you understand your character's permanent disability, you will have a better chance of intervening and casting yourself into a different part in a different play. (You may wish to reread "Is Pat Driving You Crazy?" on pages 32 and "Bozo the Chimp" on page 39.)

3. If you are the type of person who is usually sad or constantly tormented, perhaps this is your character's disposition and not yours. Once you realize this and embrace these emotions, you will be freer either to choose to remain sad and/or tormented, or to explore other emotions. (It's interesting to note that a lot of productivity, creativity, and authenticity can come from less than happy states of being.)

4. If you have become successful by using aggression, manipulation, omission, control, anger, seriousness, excessive stress, and/or tension, perhaps this is your character's way of achieving success. Once you accept this as a possibility, you will be freer to continue using these draining and confining tools, or you can explore other avenues to produce the same or better results with greater joy, trust, freedom, and relaxation.

Your main objective is to understand that there is a powerful automatic mechanism that up until now has been controlling your life. If you know where you want to go, but you can never seem to get there, look to see if your soap opera character is the one who is restraining you. By stopping and creating a little distance between yourself and your character, you will be freer to take on a more empowering part in a more inspiring play. By applying The 15 Second Principle, you can disengage from the scenario in order to rewrite and recast the play. William Shakespeare, not surprisingly, said it best (in *As You Like It*):

> *All the world's a stage, and all the men and women merely*
> *players ... And one man in his time plays many parts ...*

◆HOLD THE VISION◆

The thing has already taken form in my mind before I start it.

The first attempts are absolutely unbearable.

I say this because I want you to know that if you see something worthwhile in what I am doing, it is not by accident but because of real direction and purpose.

—Vincent Van Gogh

Very successful people can also be called creative visionaries. They have learned how to picture specific outcomes in their minds and then have developed the discipline and skills to transform these mental blueprints into realities. They have developed the capacity to hold the vision and to keep sustaining it, regardless of the barriers, detours, or emotions that might materialize. Visionaries do not let outer circumstances, such as disappointments, tragedies, setbacks, or injuries, permanently weaken their commitment to their vision. They are able to keep their dream safe and sound, like a protected eternal flame, regardless of debilitating emotions or circumstances.

Visionaries also have the ability to express themselves in positive and successful verbal pictures. In conversations (internal and external), they are constantly creating a powerful reality that supports their vision. They are comfortable speaking in terms of "when" and not "if." They have fun thinking in terms of "can" rather than "can't." They enjoy going toward something challenging more than avoiding something negative. They take full responsibility for producing their own destinies. During a children's fund-raising event, Graham Nash, of Crosby, Stills, Nash, and Young, shared his visionary process this way: "I dreamed about being a rock star at eleven, twelve, and thirteen. Then I pulled myself toward my dream."

Visionaries have a healthy relationship with disappointment and loss. While they would prefer not to experience these feelings, they are not afraid of them. They allow themselves the freedom to feel loss and to grieve, yet they don't let these emotions permanently prevent them from getting back on the path and following their dreams.

In addition to having a goal, visionaries also enjoy the journey. They value both the payoff and the path. In a sense, they live life as though they are traveling on a cruise ship. When on a cruise, while you do have a specific destination, the most important part of the trip, and what you are paying for, is the wonderful experience during the ride. It's the food, pampering, people, sunrise, sunset. Not partaking in the pleasure and amenities of the cruise and being obsessed with docking at your destination in record time would be an insane way to experience a cruise.

Visionaries have more faith and less hope. Even when they still have no tangible proof of success, they have complete confidence and trust that if they keep showing up, doing the work, and making refinements, things will be okay. They act as if they have peeked at the last page of a suspense novel and know how well things will ultimately turn out. Because of this insider information, visionaries don't struggle or panic when unfavorable circumstances appear.

Visionaries also know that suffering and excessive stress come from fretting, straddling, and procrastination, not from doing the actual work. They live more in the moment (present time) and less in past failures or future fears. Although there might be storms all around them, visionaries live in the eye of the hurricane where things are a little calmer. Their faithful stillness gives them a lot more freedom and pleasure as they pursue their goals.

Regardless of how poorly you're performing or how bleak the outlook, use The 15 Second Principle by connecting or reconnecting to your inner vision of success. When creating your successful blueprint use every one of your senses. The more specific, vibrant, and positive the pictures, colors, odors, tastes, and textures, the more powerful this visionary process will become. By being a visionary, you will develop the ability to refocus your attention, and reprogram your belief system, when things are falling apart around you. What we are talking about is the ability to feel, include, accept, regroup, and recommit during rough and devastating times. These skills will help you to revitalize your faith.

> *Until one is committed, there is hesitancy, the chance to*
> *draw back, always ineffectiveness. Concerning all acts of*
> *initiative (and creation) there is one elementary truth, the*
> *ignorance of which kills countless ideas and splendid*
> *plans: that the moment one definitely commits oneself, then*
> *providence moves too. All sorts of things occur to help one*
> *that would never otherwise have occurred. A whole stream*
> *of events from the decision, raising in one's favor all man-*
> *ner of unforeseen incidents and meetings and material*
> *assistance which no man could have dreamed would have*
> *come his way. I have learned a deep respect for one of*
> *Goethe's couplets: "Whatever you can do or dream you can,*
> *begin it. Boldness has genius, power and magic in it."*

> —W. H. Murray,
> *reporting on the Scottish*
> *Himalayan expedition*

THE SAFETY TO QUESTION

While some people go through life claiming to have many profound and life-altering epiphanies, I am, unfortunately, not one
of them. Nonetheless, I was fortunate to have experienced a single one. It was so powerful that it changed my life. I would like to
share it with you.

Just before entering college, I worked as a junior counselor at
Buck's Rock Camp. It is located in New Milford, Connecticut,
and is one of the most amazing camps in the world. I can't imagine another camp providing a more creative and intellectually
stimulating environment. The campers range in age from thirteen to seventeen and are offered an incredible array of arts,
crafts, sports, and farming activities. Its founder, Ernest Bulova, a
New York psychologist, is in his nineties and still spends his summers up there.

Each week, on the porch of the mess hall, Dr. Bulova would
give a lecture on some aspect of psychology. One week the topic
he chose was a patient of Sigmund Freud's, named Anna, who

had become paralyzed from the waist down. Even though the doctors found nothing medically wrong with her, she was still not able to walk. After she revealed her family history, Freud learned that Anna had fallen in love with her sister's fiancé and had eloped with the young man. Soon after their marriage, Anna became paralyzed.

Freud felt that there was a direct correlation between Anna's guilt and her paralysis. Through analysis, he was able to make her realize that her paralysis was her way of punishing herself both physically and sexually. Once Anna was willing to understand and deal with the cause of her paralysis, her disability rapidly disappeared.

After hearing this fascinating story, I headed back to my bunk. As I walked through the dark woods, Dr. Bulova's story kept running through my mind. *Is there a message there for me?* I wondered. I then began to think of where I might be paralyzed. I didn't have to look too far. I had been a stammerer for most of my life.*

I then asked myself the following question: *Was it possible that my stammering was also some kind of guilt-inflicted paralysis?* I knew that as the youngest child in the family, I sometimes felt unable to break the ice and speak up. Playing this scenario out further, my thoughts followed these general lines: *My stammering is a shutting down, cutting off, and blocking of my breath and speech. Why is this? Is there anything that I could be afraid of or too guilty to say (or think)?* At first, nothing clear popped into my mind. I then got more specific with this question: *What would be the most guilt-ridden and villainous thought that I could ever have?*

After racking my brain for a minute, the following thought surfaced. It regarded my family. Because we were all very close, the most shameful question I could ever invent was, "Do I really love my family?" With trembling legs and trepidation running through my body, I dared to ask the question out loud. I waited

---

* A stammer is not a stutter. A stammer feels like an electrical short circuit in the body. Everything in your body momentarily freezes (including your breathing). While in this temporary, nonverbal, shut-down state you can't utter a word or a sound. A stammer or shutdown can last for a fraction of a second to many seconds.

for lightning to strike me or for the ground to start shaking. Much to my surprise and relief, nothing happened. The woods were still peaceful and calm and I was still alive and well. It seemed this horrendous question didn't offend the universe.

As soon as I posed this question, however, an amazing physical experience took hold of me. It felt like inside my stomach there was a huge, tightly wound gray metal coil (similar to the ones that were used in old wind-up clocks, spinning tops, and toy cars). Suddenly, starting from the middle of my stomach, the center of the gray coil began to expand in geometric proportions. It grew larger than my stomach, larger than my body, larger than the path, larger than the woods, larger than Connecticut, and larger than the planet. It kept expanding out, out, out, until it disappeared into the universe.

I then experienced a physical and mental separation between myself and my family. Standing in the woods, I had the freedom and space to look at them objectively as though I were a visiting guest rather than an active participant. After deep thought and consideration about my father, mother, and sister, I began to laugh. The answer to this ominous question was a resounding yes, I did love each of them.

By allowing myself the safety to entertain any thought and to have any feeling, my speech impediment seemed to lose its hold over me. After having this primal experience, I understood that it was the fear of asking this question and not necessarily the exact answer that was freezing my speech. After this uncoiling experience, I knew that my stammering would no longer serve the function of protecting me from an unacceptable thought. I felt that at some point in the future, I was going to be cured of this affliction. Within a month of entering the University of Vermont, my actual stammering lessened appreciably. Within two months, it had almost disappeared. At long last, I was free from the visceral disability that had hounded me for all my speaking years.

If you feel like personally playing around with this topic of freedom, let me suggest three powerful questions that you might want to ask yourself and think about. The first one is, "What feelings, thoughts, and words am I not allowed to have around myself?" The second one is, "What feelings, thoughts, and words are people not allowed to have around me?" The third one is, "What feelings, thoughts, and words am I not allowed to have around certain people?"

If you discover that there are certain mental and/or physical areas that you are not allowing yourself to visit, stop and apply The 15 Second Principle. By allowing yourself a little time to venture into these uncharted territories, you will be freer to create a more open, authentic, and nurturing environment for yourself and others.

◈ THE SKILL OF FORGIVENESS ◈

Because we are human, we are all going to make mistakes. When these mishaps, transgressions, and faulty decisions occur, how are we going respond – with anger or depression, or with masterful forgiveness? How much permission are we going to give ourselves to be less than perfect? Here is a true – and tragic – story that perhaps will stretch your ability to forgive yourself and others.

Dave was a professional cameraman and skydiver from North Carolina. He was paid to videotape novice skydivers. He'd jump out of airplanes and shoot close-up footage of their exciting descents. These videos would serve both as a reminder to the jumpers and proof to their friends that they had, in fact, gone skydiving.

On one routine run, Dave and a tandem team (composed of a novice and an instructor) jumped out of a plane and began to free-fall. Dave taped the tandem's entire free-fall dive. Then, just before the release chords were supposed to be pulled, Dave freaked out and began screaming at the top of his lungs. What prompted this explosive emotional outburst was that Dave had just discovered that he had done the unthinkable. He had forgotten to take something with him – his own parachute! That's right. Apparently, he had gotten so involved with checking his video camera and helping the tandem duo prepare, that he had totally forgotten about his own equipment, safety, and needs.* As I indicated earlier, this story does not have a miraculous ending. Poor Dave did not survive the fall. His was the most serious of mistakes, and it cost him his life.

What can we learn from Dave's tragic demise? Perhaps his legacy is that his unthinkable action should set a standard for the *worst-case scenario of forgetfulness*. It would be difficult to mess up worse than Dave did. Since hearing this story, whenever I start to berate myself for a poor memory, stupid decision, or costly mistake, I now ask myself one simple question: "Okay, Al, you screwed up and it was a stupid mistake, but did you forget the parachute?" When the answer is no, I let up on myself and give myself a kinder and gentler thrashing. Scrooge, in *A Christmas Carol,* discovered this the hard way. In addition, just before leaving a place, you might pose this question, "What am I leaving behind?" This is a much more gentle and nurturing approach than "Better not forget anything!"

To be a great performer, you must be both an ultimate *demander* and an ultimate *forgiver*. Being ruthless and unforgiving is no way to treat yourself or others. Barreling through life and whipping everything that gets in your way (including yourself) is not an empowering approach. While you may produce results, the cost will be prohibitive.

Living inside of each of us is a *creator* and a *critic*. The creator yearns to create and self-express; the critic loves to stand in constant judgment. Obviously, this is a very difficult and unsafe environment for the creator to play and produce in. The creator has a very difficult time executing actions when the critic is breathing down his or her neck and whispering, "Better not screw up again, you idiot."

Living in constant fear of the critic's wrath will only limit your aliveness and spontaneity. This is a costly approach to success. Instead, give yourself permission to be human. If a scientist's experiment fails, that doesn't make the scientist a failure. Had Thomas Edison berated himself every time one of his experiments failed, we might still be reading by candlelight and using manual typewriters. Allow yourself some slack when you screw up.

---

* Dave was wearing a chest harness that contained his video pack. Apparently he had mistaken the feeling of the video harness for his parachute. Although his camera was destroyed, the videotape survived and revealed his dramatic and self-berating monologue.

This will give you a safer and more passionate environment within which to play, risk, stumble, fall, recover, heal, and succeed.

If you want to create and experience more mini-breakthroughs in your life, try not to overreact when you or a loved one makes a mistake. Instead, apply The 15 Second Principle by stopping your old knee-jerk berating behavior. Your goal is to substitute a reprimanding reactive behavior for a more nurturing one. Rather than picking up the whip, pick up the feather. Remind yourself that although your performance was perhaps embarrassing, costly, and less than stellar, you didn't forget your parachute. By letting the punishment fit the crime and the berating fit the transgression you will lead a happier and more creative life.

◆PASSION RARELY DIES◆

Every few years, I muster the courage to commit to a thorough housecleaning. This past year was that time again. I went through every object and piece of paper that I owned. It took me many weeks to accomplish this primal and challenging task. In the middle of this process, I opened a dusty old carton and discovered a favorite childhood treasure. It was a small, and magical, piece of driftwood. As I touched its sleek and shiny surface, I was suddenly transported back in time. I found myself in Peterborough, New Hampshire, at Sargent Summer Camp. There I was, a newborn teenager, sitting under a huge maple tree and sanding away at this precious object. I remembered how my most peaceful moments of that entire summer were spent smoothing out the rough edges of this special piece of wood. I recalled how naturally high I got just handling, refining, and sanding nature's beautiful gift.

I also remembered my motivations for working on the wood. It wasn't to please my parents, counselors, or girlfriend. And it wasn't for fortune or fame. It was just for me. It was a pure, personal experience. There were no ulterior motives other than pleasure. It had everything to do with feeling good and nothing to do with looking good.

As I placed the driftwood on my dresser, I began to wonder about my current relationship with wood. Several decades had passed; would I still get a kick out of working on a piece of driftwood? At that moment I remembered recently seeing a large and fascinating piece of burl wood sitting at the entrance of a garden nursery. Seizing the moment, I ran to my car and drove back down to the nursery. The piece of wood was still sitting there. I paid the owner twenty-five dollars, put it in my trunk, and drove home. After placing it on my dinette table, I took different types of tools and sandpaper and began to clean and sand my new-found friend.

Within a few minutes, an amazing thing happened. The same wood adrenaline high that I experienced decades before came rushing back. Apparently, these passionate feelings when working with wood had never died. Rather, they were buried alive and just waiting to be uncovered.

We need to trust that whatever we loved to do as children, we will most likely still love to do now (assuming a forced practicing regimen didn't beat the excitement out of us). Perhaps our personal passions are eternal, and we never outgrow the things we once loved doing.

If you want to check out this theory, make a list of all the things that you loved to do as a child. Make sure that these are hobbies that you did just for yourself. (Your list might include painting, catching and throwing a ball, molding in clay, playing music, ice skating, folk dancing, playing with a yo-yo.) Reintroduce yourself to one of these childhood interests. You just may discover that there are many passions still alive inside of you.

As you attempt to reintroduce yourself to one of your early passions, be on the alert for the passion saboteur who lives within your mind. This entity will try to discourage you from exploring your old hobbies and interests. It will usually attempt this by using one of the following tactics. First, as we have already discussed, it will convince you that your childhood passion has died. Second, it will tell you that you will never regain your earlier proficiency, so why depress and frustrate yourself? Third, it will remind you of how compulsive you are, and that once uncovered, this passion will once again take over your entire life.

If any of the above reasons enters your head, don't let it prevent you from applying The 15 Second Principle. This can be accomplished by turning down the saboteur's volume and by taking a mini-action in the direction of your buried passions.

If you are not having as much fun in life as you would like to have, perhaps it is time to dust off one of your childhood passions. When 168 hours go by (one week) and you have not scheduled at least fifteen minutes for one of your pure passions, it's time to reevaluate your priorities and lifestyle. By reawakening the wondrous childhood passions that are sleeping inside of you, you stand an excellent chance of rekindling the lost excitement and wonder of your youth.

> *Every child is an artist. The problem is how to remain an artist once he grows up.*
>
> —*Pablo Picasso*

Chasing This Thing
Called Mastery

Seek, above all, for a game worth playing. Such is the advice of the oracle to modern man. Having found the game play it with intensity – play as if your life and sanity depended on it. (They do depend on it.) Follow the example of the French existentialists and flourish a banner bearing the word "engagement." Though nothing means anything and all roads are marked "no exit," yet move as if your movements had some purpose. If life does not seem to offer a game worth playing, then invent one. For it must be clear, even to the most clouded intelligence, that any game is better than no game.

—Robert S. DeRopp
The Master Game

A realistic way to view mastery is to look at it as a never-ending odyssey. Because the human body is a source of boundless potential and infinite possibilities, the road to mastery turns out to be an eternal and enlivening journey. There will always be another nuance and plateau ahead of us, so no one ever arrives at a place called Mastery. It's somewhat like peeling an endless onion. Instead of mastery, what we are really talking about is an endless devotion to curiosity. A master is basically a passionate student who keeps showing up to learn just a little more and improve one more nuance or skill. Master-students also know that they will never graduate, nor do they want to. What keeps the master-student perpetually enrolled is the fascination with the subject matter. The Japanese have a word, *kaisen*, that comes very close to describing student-mastery: "a span of continuous and never-ending improvement." Mastery, then, is more a state of impassioned inquisitiveness than a definable point or a fixed level of proficiency.

I was blessed to have been introduced to the master-student concept at the ripe old age of thirteen. The revelation occurred one day at the Long Island Institute of Music, where I was studying music. As I was waiting for my clarinet lesson to begin, the director of the institute asked me if I was aware that I had something in common with Benny Goodman. I couldn't imagine what this brilliant musician and I had in common, so I answered, "No." The director responded that our commonality was that we were both taking lessons from my teacher, Mr. Duques.

I couldn't believe my ears. Why would the most famous clarinetist in the world still be studying? I knew that Augustin Duques was a great clarinetist (he had been the principal clarinetist in Toscanini's NBC Symphony Orchestra), but I was still quite taken aback by this fascinating piece of information. What I soon discovered was that Mr. Goodman was aware of the limitless nature of his craft, which he responded to by becoming a master-student. A master-student polishes his strong points and fortifies his weaker points. If Benny Goodman did have a weaker area, it was his classical side. To strengthen this, he sought out Mr. Duques, a master classical teacher. Perhaps Mr. Goodman just needed a set of trained classical ears to critique his playing. Or maybe he was looking for an alternative fingering, a better way of practicing scales, or a new way of improving his tone. Apparently, by placing his ego in the freezer and nurturing his inquisitive side, Benny Goodman was able to reap musical benefits from many people. This, in turn, enabled him constantly to refine his craft.

A master-student does not grab for that elusive brass ring that will always be just a little out of reach. Instead, he approaches life as though he already has the brass ring. All he is constantly doing is molding, sanding, and polishing it. Mastery is an approach, an attitude, a state of being. The master-student has a burning and impassioned inquisitiveness that keeps revitalizing him as he delves deeper and deeper into an endless world.

The master-student doesn't act on all of his feelings. Just because he feels like taking a cigarette, downing a drink, or calling his bookie, the master-student may not act on those feelings. Similarly, just because she feels like having that piece of pie, buying that new dress, or calling her ex-boyfriend who physically and emotionally abused her, the master-student doesn't necessarily put these desires into action.

Conversely, the master-student acts on things she may not feel like acting upon. From flossing one's teeth to calling a head hunter, from taking the garbage out to signing up for a course on changing careers, the master-student takes actions even though she may not feel like it.

Above all, the master-student keeps showing up. He is dedicated to working on some aspect of his chosen field until he dies. He gives himself an enormous amount of permission to fail, before he declares himself a failure. He is more committed to his word, process, and character than he is to results or feelings. He is quite patient with his progress and keeps refining his craft, not to improve or to have major breakthroughs, but because he enjoys the refinement process.

The material in this chapter is designed to improve your understanding of mastery. I have included inspirational stories, experiences, and lessons that were most helpful in enabling me to gain a deeper appreciation for this endless journey.

◆ THE MASTERY APTITUDE TEST ◆

A master-student should always be honing certain skills and personal characteristics. To help you accomplish this, I designed the Mastery Aptitude Test. It will help you to become more aware of specific mastery attributes. Each attribute can be measured on a scale from 1 to 10 (1 meaning your abilities are very weak and 10 meaning your abilities are very strong). When grading your current proficiency levels use a pencil and circle each number lightly. This will make it easier for you to retest yourself in the future.

1. A Relationship with Fear

You don't let fear stop you from pursuing your goals. If the fear doesn't go away, you take the fear with you and venture forward.

1   2   3   4   5   6   7   8   9   10

2. A Relationship with Passion

You pursue something because it interests you. While it is nice to improve, your main motivational force is curiosity and excitement.

1   2   3   4   5   6   7   8   9   10

3. A Relationship with Imperfection

You can live with imperfection (in yourself and others). You are not run by the compulsion to be perfect. Rather, you are more interested in refinement.

1   2   3   4   5   6   7   8   9   10

4. A Relationship with Rejection

You do not let rejection or negative criticism permanently stop you from pursuing your dreams. You can lick your wounds until they heal, slowly get up off the mat, and turn a mishap into a mini-breakthrough.

1   2   3   4   5   6   7   8   9   10

5. A Relationship with Commitment

You keep "showing up" because you said you would. You follow your dreams and take one more step forward, even if you don't feel like it. You have a tenacious will to follow your goals, not your feelings.

1   2   3   4   5   6   7   8   9   10

6. A Relationship with Change

You are not limited by self-imposed boundaries or immobilized by fear of change.

1   2   3   4   5   6   7   8   9   10

7. A Relationship with Curiosity
You are able to tap back into your childhood state of curiosity and wonderment.

1   2   3   4   5   6   7   8   9   10

8. A Relationship with Inertia and Stagnation
You can be stuck in the state of inertia and stagnation and slowly but surely take enough small but incremental steps to bring yourself into a state of momentum.

1   2   3   4   5   6   7   8   9   10

9. A Relationship with Actions and Activities
You can recognize the differences between an action and an activity and are in a continual state of balancing the two.

1   2   3   4   5   6   7   8   9   10

10. A Relationship with Money
You know how to attract money and when to save, spend, give, and lend it.

1   2   3   4   5   6   7   8   9   10

11. A Relationship with Procrastination
You are aware of when you are procrastinating, and you can quickly take some mini-action to break through the wall of procrastination.

1   2   3   4   5   6   7   8   9   10

12. A Relationship with Seeking Support
You can call on friends and seek their help and advice. You get feedback before making important decisions. You don't try to go it alone.

1   2   3   4   5   6   7   8   9   10

13. A Relationship with Your Vision
You can create and re-create your vision even when it appears to be unreasonable and invisible to the rest of the world.

1   2   3   4   5   6   7   8   9   10

14. A Relationship with Creativity
You create not to prove how talented you are, or to receive love or acceptance, but rather out of a need for self-expression.

1   2   3   4   5   6   7   8   9   10

15. A Relationship with Process
You give as much importance to *how* you do something (a nurturing process) as to the results of that action.

1   2   3   4   5   6   7   8   9   10

16. A Relationship with Completion
You can begin and complete projects regardless of how you feel about them. You honor your word and your verbal contracts regardless of your moods or emotions.

1   2   3   4   5   6   7   8   9   10

17. A Relationship between Giving and Receiving
Your interpersonal relationships are equally balanced between caring about others and letting others care about you.

1   2   3   4   5   6   7   8   9   10

18. A Relationship with Learning
You can create a nurturing learning environment for yourself and others in which it is safe to appear stupid and inept.

1   2   3   4   5   6   7   8   9   10

19. A Relationship with Depression
You know the difference between mild, fleeting depression and debilitating depression. You are not ashamed to seek help if and when you determine the debilitating depression is interfering with the quality of your life.

1   2   3   4   5   6   7   8   9   10

20. A Relationship with Forgiveness
You can forgive yourself (and others) when mistakes occur.

1   2   3   4   5   6   7   8   9   10

21. A Relationship with Addictions and Limiting Habits
You are aware of your addictions and are working on a daily basis to lessen your need for them. You are controlling them more than they are controlling you.

1   2   3   4   5   6   7   8   9   10

22. A Relationship with Fitness
You are enjoying the process of becoming more mentally and physically fit.

1   2   3   4   5   6   7   8   9   10

23. A Relationship with Organization
Your home and working environments are organized and you like the process of getting and staying organized.

1   2   3   4   5   6   7   8   9   10

24. A Relationship with Grieving
You give yourself permission to go through a deep grieving process. This includes the death of a loved one, divorce, and loss of a job. You also know when the time for grieving deeply is complete.

1   2   3   4   5   6   7   8   9   10

25. A Relationship with Practicing
You have fun practicing your craft and are constantly inventing new ways to make the process of practicing more efficient and enjoyable.

1   2   3   4   5   6   7   8   9   10

26. A Relationship with Disappointment

You pursue success, yet can handle the feelings that disappointment and failed attempts bring up. You do not let fear of disappointment determine how high you set your sights.

1   2   3   4   5   6   7   8   9   10

27. A Relationship with Personal Character

You can count on your own personal character regardless of the circumstances and temptations.

1   2   3   4   5   6   7   8   9   10

Before reading further, please add up your total score. Your total score can range from 27 to 270.

Student-Mastery Score: _____

The Mastery Aptitude Test Score

If you haven't guessed already, I'm not at all interested in how high or low your student-mastery score is – and neither should you be. The purpose of this test was not to compare your scores with the rest of the world's. Neither was it designed to have you feel good or bad about yourself. Rather, it was created to expand your self-awareness of these masterful attributes. Ultimately, you will have to decide how important each attribute is for you. Then the question becomes: How proficient do you want to become with each characteristic?

It would be helpful every now and then to return to this aptitude test. First, it will refresh your memory as to what the twenty-seven relationships are, and second, you can observe whether you are expanding or contracting in each area. Because you are only human, each time you revisit this list, you will most likely be improving in some areas and retreating in others. In fact, at times, your total master-student scores might even be going down. What is most important is that you become more aware of these skills and disciplines and work toward improving your relationship with them. This enhanced sensitivity will improve your chances of becoming a more human and fully integrated person.

ALEXANDER GODUNOV'S
APPROACH TO MASTERY

This past weekend, I happened to tune in to a television program on Alexander Godunov. Along with being a wonderful actor, he was one of the greatest, most passionate, and virile ballet dancers that the Soviet Union ever produced. Included in the program was a film clip in which Alexander jumped high into the air, did two 360-degree turns, and then effortlessly descended to the wooden floor. When he landed on the stage, he was perfectly balanced and facing directly toward the audience. It was an inspiring feat to view. The question one might ask about his accomplishment is, Did he have to pray before taking that leap, or had he mastered it? At that moment, I smiled because I knew the answer. It was mastery.

I knew the answer because a few years before his untimely and shocking death, I had witnessed him execute two of those same double 360s in less than ideal circumstances. For many years, I had the privilege of being Alexander's tennis coach. One day while on the court, we were discussing where the leaping power should come from when a tennis player jumps in the air in order to hit an overhead smash. Alexander told me that it was the heel of the foot that gave him the power to do his double 360-degree ballet turns. I immediately stopped him. "Do you mean you can just stand there, jump directly up into the air, and do two 360-degree turns?" With a very modest and boyish expression on his face, he answered, "Yes." I asked him if he would do the jump right there in front of me. After *much* pleading and begging (he hated showing off), he finally agreed to execute the move.

Alexander handed me his tennis racquet, looked me straight in the eyes, and then effortlessly lifted off the ground and appeared skyward bound. I was fascinated at how relaxed his face and body appeared. While defying gravity, he easily executed his two 360-degree turns before gracefully returning to the same exact spot. Because I had trouble believing my eyes, he was generous enough to repeat the jump in a perfect fashion.

While I'm sure Alexander would have preferred his ballet slippers, leotards, wooden floor, full orchestra, and a theater filled with a thousand appreciative fans, he did not need these elements to execute the jump. He understood the movement so well that he could create it perfectly in spite of a less than ideal dancing environment – tennis shoes, warm-up pants, a hard cement surface, and an audience of one.

What I learned from Alexander was that someone who truly understands a sport, art form, or skill can perform well in less than perfect circumstances. As an example, because we understand the actions of tying our shoelaces so well, we can still tie them outdoors regardless of the weather conditions, in rain, sleet, or snow.

An even more fascinating part of working with Alexander, however, was how he treated the entire learning process. Because he was a beginner who took many lessons (he had five private lessons per week for several years), I saw him making thousands of mistakes. I was amazed that after producing each error, he would never get angry or impatient with himself. He never seemed to take any of the mistakes personally.

You would think that someone who had achieved world-class status in ballet would be a perfectionist and very demanding of himself in every area of his life. What I discovered was something quite the contrary. Whenever he would make an error, he would laugh, shrug his shoulders, and immediately become very detached about the error. He reacted as though the mistake had occurred hours before and that someone else had committed it.

So think of Alexander whenever you get too serious or demanding of yourself. When you get angry for producing imperfect results, unless you are a brain surgeon, lighten up a bit. This is where The 15 Second Principle can come in handy. It can help you to stop and create a little emotional distance between yourself and the imperfection. With this detachment, it is less likely that you will give extra importance to the mistake. This, in turn, will provide a safer environment for you to continue to risk, experiment, fail, forgive, regroup, and succeed. (Remember "The Skill of Forgiveness" on page 114.)

I'd like to add one additional observation about Alexander. Out of all the tennis lessons he took, he never showed up late – or even on time. Rather, he always arrived early. He revealed to me that one time the musical conductor of his ballet company in the Soviet Union showed up late for a dress rehearsal, and this conductor was not allowed to work for several years.

◆LARRY BIRD'S SUCCESS PROGRAMMING◆

We are what we repeatedly do.
Excellence, then, is not an act, but a habit.

—Aristotle

I'm always fascinated when watching assembly-line robots do their jobs. In a rhythmic and methodical fashion, they keep repeating the same precise and accurate actions time after time. They never get exhausted, bored, or overwhelmed. Instead, they seem to bring a renewed commitment and energy to each action they perform. In addition, they don't have an emotional value system that prefers one action above another. Nor are they thinking, "Just two million more bolts in the chassis and I can take an early retirement package."

While we never want to become robotlike by losing our feelings, humanity, and soul, we can learn an important lesson by observing these machines as they operate. Robots have only been programmed for success. Errors are therefore the exception rather than the rule. Robots are not fighting any bad habits, rebelling against imperfect parents, or recovering from early psychological traumas. Because they don't bring any limiting past history or current "mind chatter" with them, they are "free" to perform the functions that they were designed to execute in an efficient and effortless fashion.

There is a wonderful story about Larry Bird, one of the greatest basketball players of all time, that deals with success programming. No one in professional basketball loved practicing more than Larry Bird. He was renowned for his passionate shooting schedule. What Larry Bird lacked in talent he made up for in skill and technique. He could practice one specific shot for hours at a time. He loved to repeat a shot until there was no mystery or luck left to it. His body understood a twenty-foot shot as clearly as a three-foot shot.

The story goes that one day Larry was hired to perform in a Nestlé Crunch candy bar commercial. The script called for someone to distract him by biting into a noisy Crunch bar just as he was about to shoot. The loud crunch sound was supposed to cause him to miss the shot. The filming session took much longer than expected because Larry kept making the shot! Even though he genuinely tried to miss, his success-programmed body just didn't know how to accomplish this. Regardless of what the director told Larry or what Larry told himself, he kept sinking each basket. He was quite apologetic and embarrassed about all of his unintentionally successful shots. Eventually, after much effort, Larry was able to miss a few baskets.

Most of us aren't as skilled or perfectionistic as Larry Bird, but the more we practice and the more technique we develop, the easier and more rewarding our lives can become. Ultimately, it should be easier to produce a successful result than an unsuccessful one. Because positive programming will only occur after producing thousands of correct repetitions, the practice sessions should be enjoyable and geared to the personality and needs of each person. This will encourage us to practice even more as we develop proper physical grooving.

In addition, after practicing a specific stroke, singing a certain note, learning a new movement, fingering a new chord on a musical instrument, etc., we must have patience for this action to be absorbed organically by our bodies. More often than not, it can take months or years before the action becomes organic and we "own" it.

One of the dividends of physical grooving is emotional grooving. Emotional grooving deals with such things as confidence, trust, and faith. The more physically proficient we become (by practicing and preparing), the easier it will be to calm and refocus ourselves when doubts, fears, and distractions begin to creep into our minds.

Be aware that when practicing, at some point there will be an inner voice that will try to convince you that you have practiced enough. Whenever you hear this voice, apply The 15 Second Principle by adding just a few more repetitions. See if you can go just a little further than you think you can or want to go. Remember, just as there is a second wind in running, there is also a second wind in practicing. If you do decide to listen to this voice and stop your session, make sure the voice is coming from your masterful side and not your avoider side, which is often lazy, threatened, and rebellious. (Recall "Is Pat Driving You Crazy?" on page 32.)

> *If an unusual necessity forces us onward, a surprising thing occurs. The fatigue gets worse up to a certain point, when, gradually or suddenly, it passes away and we are fresher than before! We have evidently tapped a new level of energy. There may be layer after layer of this experience, a third and fourth "wind."*
>
> *We find amounts of ease and power that we never dreamed ourselves to own, sources of strength habitually not taxed, because habitually we never push through the obstruction of fatigue.*
>
> —*William James*

◆DON'T FOLLOW YOUR FEELINGS— FOLLOW YOUR DREAMS◆

> *Perhaps the most valuable result of all education is the ability to make yourself do the thing you have to do, when it ought to be done, whether you like it or not.*
> —*Thomas Henry Huxley*

Following your dreams and getting married are very similar experiences. Both require that you remain committed to your agreements after the "honeymoon" is over. Once the initial highs begin to ebb, and some earthly realities settle in, what then? How do you respond when your dream project encounters its first major setback? How do you react when your new spouse appears less like a perfect angel and more like an extraterrestrial? Do you stay committed to your dream or relationship and attempt to work things out, or do you immediately head west?

While passion is a powerful motivator to help us begin a dream project, it is rarely strong enough to carry us over the finishing line. To reach our goals requires skills that go way beyond enthusiasm, energy, and bliss. When the going gets tough and we encounter problems, when we experience exhaustion, depression, and feelings of helplessness, we need to be able to regroup, dig down even deeper, and take corrective actions. If you are having trouble pursuing your dreams or completing important projects, look to see if you are relying on pure excitement and the right creative mood as your main motivational forces. Are you beginning that report, practicing that instrument, writing that novel, going to the gym, or staying committed to new eating habits only when you feel like it?

If your emotions and physical states are determining when and where you devote time to a dream project or precious idea, you will need a backup emergency system for when your passion begins to wane. Fortunately (or unfortunately), the most powerful backup system available is *your word*. When you are not able to create from a magical or blissful "zone," your commitment, persistence, and integrity must take over. It's like a tag team wrestling event or relay race. Whenever your passion takes a hike, your word must be honored more than your current feelings.

This is where The 15 Second Principle can be very helpful. Whenever you catch yourself shying away from an action that you know you should be taking, but don't feel like taking, stop and ask yourself the following question: Is my commitment to this present feeling more important than my commitment to my dream? Most of the time the answer will be no.

Make room for these feelings and allow yourself to feel all of these emotions and body sensations (apathy, ambivalence, hopelessness, and/or exhaustion). Your next step is to take one more step in the direction of your dream. (Remember "The Inclusion Factor" discussed on page 29.) Even if this mini-action feels like it will be worthless or meaningless, take the action anyway. This seemingly minuscule mini-action can have an enormous impact on helping you to break through the veil of inertia. Once this occurs it will be easier to regain your mobility and momentum.

In the area of mundane tasks, when we don't feel like doing something it's usually because we have attached a perception of pain to it. It's not the action itself that is painful; rather it's the psychic pain we attach to the action. It's what the action represents to us and not the energy expended that will cause us to stay away from it. That's why making our bed can be more painful than putting a ski rack on the car. That's why getting our taxes organized can be more strenuous than playing an intense set of tennis, pumping iron, or running in the park.

As long as we are discussing feelings, let's discuss addictions for a minute. When an addiction is screaming out to be satisfied, it will be sending out a very convincing and loud message. The message, however, is a lie. The addiction will be selling the idea that there is only one solution to satisfy the yearning. It will tell you that the only way to quell your craving is to take the drink, do the drugs, smoke the cigarette, or eat the food right now. It will attempt to convince you that nothing else will quench your thirst or calm your yearning, except doing your addiction. Fortunately, for us, this is just not true. There are other options.

Consider a mosquito bite that is pleading to be scratched. At that uncomfortable moment, the bite will convince you that nothing else can ease the itching except a quality scratch. However, there are other actions available. There is anti-itch lotion, an ice cube, putting your attention somewhere else, calling a friend for support, or daring to do nothing. In this case, taking no action, and waiting for the discomfort to subside, is an empowering action.

Here's how you can apply this nonaction approach. When an addiction is calling out to you, dare to take no action for 15 seconds. Then, keep applying your nonaction 15 second agreement, for an additional 15 seconds. Keep doing this again and again and again. Ultimately, your mission is to continue these 15 second nonactions until the urge subsides. This is essentially the ability to go cold turkey, 15 seconds at a time.

Mastery is not about relying solely on zest and fervor to reach your destination. Rather, it's about being more committed to your word, dreams, and life than you are to your doubts, fears, and ambivalence. What we are talking about is the ability to be "unreasonable." While your feelings and addictions will try to convince you with their own reasons, you must have the courage to supersede their logic, do a self-intervention and become unreasonable.

What this all amounts to is your developing the ability to take corrective actions and to steer your ship toward your destination, regardless of the weather conditions, your emotional state, or the addictive sirens singing onshore. Once your dreams and goals develop into nonnegotiable agreements, your debilitating feelings, low-energy states, internal conversations, feelings of insanity, and addictive throbbings will have less control over your destiny. Ultimately, nurturing our bodies and souls must become more important than feeding our addictions.

> *Nothing in the world can take the place of persistence.*
> *Talent will not; nothing is more common than unsuccessful men*
>   *with talent.*
> *Genius will not; unrewarded genius is almost a proverb.*
> *Education alone will not; the world is full of educated derelicts.*
> *Persistence and determination alone are omnipotent.*
>   *—Calvin Coolidge*

◆ BERRY GORDY'S DOUBLE SKILLS OF WEALTH ◆

Berry Gordy is a legend in the music industry. As the creator of Motown Records, he was directly responsible for bringing us artists such as Michael Jackson, Diana Ross, the Temptations, Stevie Wonder, and Smokey Robinson. His business accomplishments, creativity, and artistic instincts are respected throughout the world.

One weekday morning several years ago, Berry and I were playing a friendly but competitive game of tennis on his private court. He lives on a magnificent estate in Bel Air. When you pass through his gates, you know that you have entered a very special world. When we finished our game, at around eleven o'clock, he picked up the phone and requested some fresh orange juice and melon. In a few minutes, a member of his staff brought down a huge silver tray containing our delicious chilled refreshments.

As we sat there, I looked around his palatial estate and realized that he had created a gorgeous minihotel all for himself. At this point, I turned to him and said, "Berry, this is an amazing way to live. You've made an incredible life for yourself here." After graciously thanking me for the compliment, he said that creating this type of lifestyle really required two skills. The first was the skill of learning how to attract, earn, and invest the money. The second skill was learning how to enjoy it. He went on to say that both skills were different. He felt that just being able to make the money didn't necessarily mean that you would ever learn how to use it for a source of pleasure and rejuvenation. He believed that most people get so caught up in making and worrying about their money that they never develop the skills to enjoy it. Since he was having a wonderful time at his mansion late on a weekday morning, it was apparent to me that he had mastered both skills.

As I exited his property through a long and beautifully manicured private driveway, his words kept echoing in my head. Both skills really do need to be worked on and developed separately. Relentless motivation might allow us to accumulate wealth (assuming, of course, the excessive pressure and stress doesn't kill us), but this drive is the very thing that can prevent us from ever stopping, relaxing, and actually smelling the roses that are on our own property. Mastery is about balancing these two challenging areas of life.

To achieve harmony between both work and play, we must continue making adjustments and corrections. By either working too hard or playing too hard, we have the capacity to derail this precariously balanced train. In a sense, what we are talking about here is the skill of self-intervention. Neither the workaholic nor the play-a-holic is free to choose other avenues in large enough doses. While they may visit other paths for a while, many of these people will return to their more familiar yet less masterful behavior.

Every now and then, stop and apply The 15 Second Principle by asking yourself whether you are flexing your work, family, and play muscles enough. Ideally, we want to be seeking a balanced blend of creativity and rejuvenation in all three areas of our lives. While few of us will ever get to live like Berry Gordy, all of us can learn to enjoy more of the blessings, health, relatives, friends, and possessions that we do have.

◆BEVERLY HILL'S SIX-POINT INTERSECTION◆

In Los Angeles, across the street from the famous Beverly Hills Hotel and one block south of Sunset Boulevard, there is a challenging intersection. Three streets, Lomitas, Beverly, and Canon, all cross each other. What makes this intersection unique is that it is very busy, yet it doesn't have any traffic lights. Instead, there are six stop signs followed by a huge and unmarked open area. Each driver, after stopping, enters this open common area and proceeds to hook up with his or her desired street. During an average day, thousands of cars weave and crisscross as each driver navigates this active, free-for-all intersection.

An interesting piece of historical data about this potentially dangerous crossroad is that no one living in the neighborhood (including the Beverly Hills Police Department) can ever remember an accident occurring there. One day, I spent an hour watching hundreds of cars enter and leave the intersection. Let me share my observations with you. As drivers enter the common area, they tend to do the following:

1. They respect the potential danger and become more alert, focused, and attentive (especially in rush-hour traffic). They shift their attention from automatic pilot to living in present time.

2. The drivers stop their secondary activities (talking on the phone, changing a cassette, singing, looking at the scenery, putting on mascara, memorizing a monologue for acting class, etc.).

3. They assume that other drivers will do something unpredictable and dangerous. Drivers take full respon-sibility for their own safety and become more attuned to the surroundings.

We can learn an important performing lesson from this six-point intersection. Whenever we are doing something that is potentially dangerous, we should show respect for our lives and endeavors by refocusing our attention and living in present time. This includes such actions as cutting with a knife, hammering a nail, shaving with a razor, climbing a ladder, driving a car (all the time). If you want the world to be a safer place for you and others, don't be preoccupied and assume that your skill, God, and luck will protect you. Rather, be fully present when you are executing potentially hazardous actions, and fewer things will go wrong. By zoning in (living in the present) rather than zoning out (mentally drifting into the past or future), you will bring more proficiency and enjoyment to your actions.*

Be aware that accidents also can occur when we simultaneously execute the potentially dangerous action and compliment ourselves on how well we are performing. If you ever find yourself performing and critiquing at the same time, stop the internal dialogue and refocus your attention back onto the action. Simply put, when you are cutting vegetables, cut the vegetables. When you are shaving, shave. When you are skiing, ski. By saving the compliments or criticism for a later date, you will have fewer accidents.

What would our lives be like if our daily concentration and involvement always resembled the six-point intersection focus? What if we had the skills to sustain this aliveness and focus for extended periods of time? What if we could become as fully engaged in our lives as Tiger Woods was when he broke all golf records at the 1997 Masters? What if paying attention took on an entirely new and energizing meaning? Obviously, the answer is

---

* Have you ever been driving somewhere and then suddenly thought, *How in the world did I get here?* If so, you mentally, 'zoned out' at some point during the journey. Have you ever gotten into your car and thought, *Did I lock the front door of the house?* If you actually had locked it, you mentally zoned out as you were doing so.

that we would be experiencing more richness, meaning, appreciation in every aspect of our lives.

The first step in this process is to become aware of when you are fully attentive and when you are not. Developing this awareness is crucial. If you catch yourself zoning out, the next step is to apply The 15 Second Principle by executing a quick sensory action. By using any one of your senses, you can immediately return to living in present time. Sensory actions might include taking a deep breath in and then gently and slowly releasing it; focusing your eyes on an object (including someone else's eyes) and observing how many colors you can see; touching an object and letting yourself be affected by its texture and temperature; listening to the tones of someone's voice; and attempting to smell the fragrances of your environment. Whenever you want to experience life to its fullest, apply these corrective sensorial actions. This discipline will help you to experience a heightened state of safety, spontaneity, and aliveness.

MASTERS OF "RELAXATION"

Sometimes, important words get so overused that they begin to lose their meaning. Unfortunately, the word *relaxation* is one of them. It has become so watered down that it has lost a lot of its usefulness. Everyone relates to the word differently, and most of the time relaxation is dealt with as a general concept. The problem is that very few people think of the expression *to relax* as an action verb. If you are tense or in a tailspin, you actually need to do something specific in order to free yourself from the situation. Just telling yourself to relax will not provide you with the needed relief that you are seeking.

This problem can be remedied by substituting a new action word in the place of relaxation. I call it *relaxion*. Relaxion is the physical and mental execution of specific actions that result in a heightened state of relaxation. In other words, relaxion is the *action* that will cause you to relax. The following stories and techniques will give you a better understanding and appreciation for the art of relaxion.

A Lesson from Johnny Carson

The king of television, Johnny Carson is also a master of relaxion. Before his retirement from *The Tonight Show*, the *Hollywood Reporter*, in a collector's series, published a 150-page tribute to him. Below are four celebrity quotes that specifically compliment him on his "hosting" skills.

> *Johnny has that quality of cradling you into that chair and making you feel comfortable and confident so that you'd deliver the best of yourself. He made me a lot more entertaining than I otherwise might have been. My only gripe for years was his suggestion that I shoe-polish my hair, that dirty rotten son of a bitch.*
>
> —*Mike Wallace*

> *The first time I was on his show was the thrill of my life. It meant that I was accepted into the elite. You knew you could trust Johnny. It's like if your daughter wants to marry a boy who you know is OK and would take care of her. Johnny's like that – you know he's going to take care of you.*
>
> —*George Foreman*

> *What's amazing about Johnny is that when he's tuned into you he gives you 100%. He has a way of getting to you with that voice of his that I've been listening to since I was 8 years old – it floats and is surreal. He's so reassuring that you come forward.*
>
> —*Dana Carvey*

> *Johnny has the incredible ability to make everybody feel comfortable. Besides his dry sense of humor and his wit, his ability to make his guests feel comfortable is the key to his success. He also never puts himself first.*
>
> —*Johnny Bench*

The only way for Johnny Carson to have made his guests feel so comfortable was for him to have been in a relaxed and safe state himself. This enabled him to become a life raft onto which all of his guests could climb, leap, or crawl. Thus buoyed and support- ed by Johnny, his guests were able to open up and do their best work. Perhaps Johnny's ability to create a safe harbor was one of the reasons that no other talk show host was able to dethrone "the king." In addition to his incredible wit and talent, Johnny Carson's relaxion skills were superior to anyone else's.

A Lesson from Dick Clark

When my tennis video first came out, the distributors requested my presence at the VSDA Video Convention in Washington, D.C. While there, I had the opportunity to demonstrate some of my tennis techniques. Inside our booth, we set up a small net and backdrop, which enabled me to stage some tennis demonstra- tions. Just before my show was to begin, Dick Clark and a video crew suddenly appeared. As it turned out, we had been selected as one of the interesting booths that Dick Clark wanted to tape. He and I talked for about a minute before the cameras began to roll. I found him to be extremely relaxed and personable. Then, a second before the taping began, something very interesting happened. When it counted the most, Dick Clark became even more relaxed, present, and open. He appeared more comfort- able and at ease with the camera on than off. Like a warm stick of butter, he became even softer as he let any residual tension melt away. It was fascinating how, on command, he was able to create a more magical and trusting zone.

A Lesson from Gary Collins

A similar thing happened when I was invited to present my teach- ing concepts and book, *Ultimate Tennis,* on *The Gary Collins Show.* Gary and I happened to arrive at the television studio at the same time. He appeared extremely tired. (He had been taping for many weeks without taking a break.) Even during a quick run- through with him, I was surprised at how low his energy and excitement levels were. However, once the show began and I joined him onstage, I was amazed at how high the level of his energy, alertness, and enthusiasm now were. It was obvious that Gary had merely been saving his energy for when he needed it the most – the real performance. Here was another nuance to the art of relaxion. There are high and low energy levels within the relaxed state, and Gary Collins was conserving his energy by remaining in a relaxed/low-energy state. At show time, though, he was able to switch into a relaxed/high-energy state. His relaxion skills enabled him to conserve his energy.

Messieurs Clark, Collins, and Carson have logged in thousands of hours in front of audiences and cameras. Their lives have revolved around either preparing for or being in front of the camera. This enormous amount of time has given them a fantastic opportunity to master their relaxion skills. Day in and day out, decade after decade, these men have been able to polish their special skills. Under the added pressure of performing, they have developed the ability to relax even more. This skill creates a heightened state of aliveness, which in turn helps their comfort, listening, trusting, and spontaneity.

While there are no instant ways to add more relaxion to your living and performing skills, below are a few specific actions that might help you to begin.

1. Always assume that your body is carrying around excess tension. This is especially true before, during, and after a performance. The residual tension can reside in any area of your body. Because most people don't have the time or interest to check out every part of their body, let me offer a few of the most important areas. These are the gateways to relaxion. Investigate the forehead, eyes, jaw, lips, back of the neck, shoulders, fingers, and stomach. Attempt to let go of any tension that may be in these parts of the body. It is vital to check out one area at a time. This is a challenging exercise because many people feel that they will look too tired and unattractive when in this relaxed state. The reality is that unless you begin from a relaxed and open state, too much tension will form when you are put under any type of pressure. The result will be an excess of stress in the body.

2. Become more aware of your breathing patterns (including the habit of holding your breath). When most people get tense and/or nervous, their breathing either stops or gets shallow (short and fast). The first step to relaxion is awareness. Ultimately, you want to be able to keep breathing in a continuous and soothing flow, even when the stakes are high and the pressure is intense. Like an Olympic swimmer doing laps, you want to be breathing either in or out rather than holding your breath for long periods of time. (See the section called "Scuba Breathing on Land" on page 150.)

3. In addition to focusing your attention and sending energy directly out to the audience (through your eyes and heart), your mission is also to create an engulfing energy. To produce engulfing energy, imagine that you have a pair of invisible elastic arms. These arms are so long that they are capable of surrounding, protecting, and hugging your entire audience (regardless of how large or small). Just like Johnny Carson, your embracing and hosting energy can create a safe harbor for yourself and your audience.

4. If you are not relaxed, it is probably because you are not living fully in present time. To get back to the present, and away from the future or past, start consciously using more of your senses. Look into the eyes of your friend or customer and attempt to see how many different colors you can see. Allow your finger pads to feel the temperature and texture of an object. Let your sensation of that object affect you. Smell the fragrances around you. Taste your lips, a breath freshener, or food. All of these relaxion sensory actions will immediately bring you back to living and performing in present time. Once in present time, you will improve your chances of being relaxed.

5. Start performing on a more regular basis. At first, choose a safer and less threatening environment for yourself. Make sure the stakes are lower than usual. Whether it's selling, asking people out on dates, public speaking, teaching, sporting,

or acting, you must work out more regularly. Performing once every three months is not going to give you enough time to experiment in the art of relaxion. Unfortunately, a sporadic performing schedule will usually produce unpredictable and/or uncomfortable results. Therefore, *keep showing up*. Eventually, getting up to perform can become a safe, fun, and energizing thing to do.

Remember that relaxation is the result of executing specific actions. If you are nervous or not performing up to your full potential, stop and apply The 15 Second Principle by using specific relaxion actions. The more specific and refined the action, the more relaxed and focused you will become. This, in turn, will improve your chances of consistently creating more ultimate performances.

◆THE DOOR PROCESS◆

> *What will determine your success in life is the level of discomfort (brought on by challenges) that you are able to become comfortable with.*
>
> —*Al Secunda*

Part of the mastery process is to become more aware of our weaker areas and to have the interest and courage to improve upon them. By strengthening our weakest links, we can become stronger, more balanced and self-fulfilled. However, discovering these weak links, and fortifying them, can become a little tricky. To help us locate and work on our most vulnerable areas, I created the door process.

Imagine you are standing in the middle of a huge lobby. On each of the four lobby walls there are many doors. Each door, which represents the entryway to a challenging aspect of life, has a descriptive title over it. The doors lead to individual rooms where you will begin to work on different aspects of your life.

While the titles are unique for each person, some of the most popular ones are: Physical Fitness, Financial Independence, Changing Careers, Intimacy and Empathy, Learning a Sport or Musical Instrument, Handling Addictions, and Following a Dream.

What you will discover is that while some doors are easy to approach and walk through, others will be much more difficult. Whenever you approach a door and hear your body and mind scream, *"Not that one!* I'll walk through any door but *not that one!"* it would be wise to investigate why you have such an aversion to that specific door. What is behind it that seems so threatening? (Remember "Homeostasis" on page 23.) More often than not, the *"not that one"* door is the very door the master-student needs to walk through.*

My most challenging door process occurred in 1977 when I moved from New York City to Southern California. I left show business behind and began teaching tennis full time. To say that I had become consumed by tennis was an understatement. I was obsessed. In addition, the more I learned, the more I wanted to share. My dream became to share my insights and discoveries by writing an instructional tennis book. This mission brought up two major hurdles. First, I had no skills in personal dream realization. While I had been able to achieve results for my parents, teachers, professors, and bosses, I didn't have any experience at pursuing and achieving the dreams that were closest to my heart.

Second, while my passion for tennis ran extremely high, my skills at writing a tennis book ran very low. I didn't think I was a very good writer. I couldn't sit still or be alone for long periods of time. I had forgotten how to type. I had never played professional tennis, nor was I a gifted athlete. I wasn't sure of how to share the information. I was always tired after long days of teaching. I couldn't imagine an agent and publisher being interested in my manuscript. I was scared to death to face something that meant so much to me.

---

* If the door process doesn't feel right for you at this time, don't force yourself into one of these challenging rooms. Instead, revisit this material at a later date, and see if it feels more appropriate for you.

Obviously, I felt very overwhelmed and ill-equipped. To help me face this challenge, I created this thing called The 15 Second Agreement. Each day I would ask myself this question: "Even though I'm scared to death, can I at least face the writing for a minimum of 15 seconds?" And, when it applied: "Even though I didn't write yesterday, am I willing to forgive myself?" These were the only two agreements that I ever made regarding my book.

Sometimes there would be weeks on end where I couldn't write a word. When this occurred, I would keep stretching my forgiveness muscle. What I discovered was that the sooner I could truly forgive myself, the sooner I was able to return to writing (for a minimum of 15 seconds).

I also must admit that breaking through the inertia and committing to my 15 Second Agreement was extremely confrontational. Rather than being a joyous or flowing experience, the first 15 seconds often seemed like a life-or-death struggle. Moving my project forward often felt like I was driving a car by simultaneously pressing down on both the accelerator and the brake pedal. The accelerator represented my passion, and the brake all my fears. My only saving grace was that my passion was just a little stronger than my fears. This allowed me, slowly but surely, to inch my way down the road. Also, the longer I stayed behind the wheel, the stronger the accelerator became and the weaker the brakes became.

Well, after living with The 15 Second Agreement for seven years, something miraculous happened. I actually completed a rough draft of my book. I then found a Los Angeles agent who loved my unique tennis approach. Several months later he sold the book to Simon & Schuster. In addition, the celebrity community related so much to my passion, perseverance, and teaching style that the book was endorsed by Billie Jean King, Stan Smith, Walter Cronkite, James Coburn, and Bruce Jenner. *Ultimate Tennis* is currently in its ninth printing.

I bring up the history of my journey in the hopes that it will inspire you. I'm here to tell you that if I could accomplish this feat, with so little confidence and so few skills, you too can achieve amazing results. The most empowering way to go about this is to have your dreams become more important than the perceived and/or real discomfort that you will experience. Your will to keep following your dream must be greater than your fear. Ideally, your commitment and will should be generated from a creative and playful place rather than a fearful survival mode.

The door process encourages you intentionally to alter your relationship with the weaker areas of your life. It invites you to walk through the doors in order to activate and experience the discomfort. Instead of attempting to eradicate the feelings, conquer the fear, or withstand the pain, your intention is to enter one of these rooms in order to engage, explore, and experience the very feelings you have been afraid to feel. The more you can surrender to and expand your capacity to be with the physical and emotional discomfort, the less disabling these feelings will tend to become. Barbara Walters, on one of her shows, asked Woody Harrelson why he selected acting as a profession. "Because I was terrified of it," was his answer. It's obvious from his response that Harrelson has an engaging and empowering relationship with discomfort and fear.

Upon entering one of these challenging rooms, the best thing to do is to relax and allow the discomfort to permeate your body. You want to become more comfortable with the uncomfortable. In addition, it's best not to give these feelings any extra meaning and importance by connecting them to past or future stories, images, or events. It is when you attach these feelings to childhood memories, past failures, or future nightmares that you create the fear. The skill is to isolate these uncomfortable sensations and to experience them as unlabeled experiences occurring in present time. Your goal is just to feel the feelings and nothing more. This approach will prevent the discomfort from turning into a debilitating fear. In addition, the greater your capacity for the discomfort, the less debilitating the sensations will become.

Entering one of these rooms and walking into a cold pond are quite similar. Upon entering the pond our first instinct is usually to brace our bodies and to use tension to protect ourselves from the cold water. This, however, rarely eases the discomfort. It's only by relaxing our shoulders, fingers, and jaw and by breathing continuously that we can expand our capacity to be with the discomfort. Once we become more comfortable with the discomfort, the experience can shift from horrendous to invigorating.

Be aware that once we cross the threshold and enter one of these rooms, more often than not we will be overwhelmed. Because we have had aversions to these areas, it is natural for us to feel like ill-equipped beginners. Therefore, be prepared to have feelings of incompetence as your helpless internal voice screams, "It's too late!" "I'm too old!" "Get me out of here!" "I don't have any talent!" "It's impossible!" and "I'd rather be in jail than master this thing!"

The simplest way to deal with this frightened novice voice is to make room for its opinion while not being ruled by it. You want to include it in the general mix of opinions while not focusing your attention directly on it. (Refer back to "The Inclusion Factor" on page 29.) Ultimately, this voice needs to be loved yet treated like an insane adviser who has fallen out of favor.

The door process is perhaps the most challenging aspect of this book. To attempt the dreams we cherish the most. To seek out the things that frighten us the most. To talk about things we'd prefer not to talk about. To ask the questions we are afraid to ask. To dare to feel worthy and make requests of others. To expand the dynamics and possibilities of our conversations. All of these things will require an enormous amount of courage and character. However, in order to realize our dreams or to delve into the world of mastery, we will have to visit unfamiliar realms, which will generate uncomfortable feelings. The more we can shift our relationship with these uncomfortable realms and actually choose the areas that simultaneously are attracting and scaring us, the more empowering and less debilitating these settings and sensations will become. Through them we will then be able to achieve more freedom, satisfaction, self-respect, and balance. Utimately, the joy and discomfort that we will encounter by pursuing our dreams must become more important than the safety and suffering we will experience by not pursuing them.

Whether small or great, and no matter what the stage or grade of life, the Call rings up the curtain, always on a mystery of transfiguration – on a rite, or moment, of spiritual

*passage, which, when complete, amounts to a dying and a
rebirth. The familiar life horizon has been outgrown; the
old concepts, ideals, and emotional patterns no longer fit;
the time for the passing of a threshold is at hand.*

—Joseph Campbell
(*in Michael Toms's* An Open Life)

◆ARTHUR ASHE'S ADAPTABILITY◆

If you are reading this book, there is an excellent chance that you
are interested in success. Usually success-oriented people are the
ones who want to become even more effective. Unless you won
the lottery or were born into wealth, chances are you pursue success by producing results. You have developed certain skills that
you constantly draw upon to achieve your goals. The more you
use these skills, the more refined your production techniques
have become. I'd like to share an important story that might shed
some additional light on performing excellence.

The date was July 5, 1975. The place was Wimbledon, England.
Arthur Ashe and Jimmy Connors were about to meet each other in
the finals of the most prestigious tennis event in the world. The
odds in Las Vegas heavily favored Connors. Jimmy had won
Wimbledon the previous year, and he had never lost to Ashe (3–0).
In addition, Jimmy hadn't dropped one set in the entire tournament (six previous matches). In the semifinals, Connors had
crushed Roscoe Tanner 6–4, 6–1, 6–4. Tanner had one of the fastest
and most devastating serves in the game. Jimmy handled his powerful serve with ease. On a grass service, this is extremely difficult. The
harder Roscoe served the ball, the faster Jimmy returned it. It was
apparent to everyone that Connors was playing brilliant tennis.

Ashe, on the other hand, had had a little more difficulty in his
ascent to the finals. In the semifinals he'd outlasted Tony Roche
5–7, 6–4, 7–5, 8–9, 6–4. While it wasn't smooth sailing, Arthur's
main weapons – a fast serve, powerful ground strokes, and great
volleys – had kept coming through for him.

At some point, just before the finals began, a reality jolted
Ashe. He realized that he was going to lose to Connors if he used

the same strokes and strategies that had got him to the finals. He would once again come up short if he pitted his strengths against Connors's. Jimmy would take Arthur's power and turn it against him.

It was at this point that Ashe had the courage to become adaptive. He abandoned his usual way of winning because it was not appropriate for this specific situation. He exchanged an offensive strategy for a defensive one by replacing a power game with a risky game of finesse. Rather than trying to overwhelm Jimmy with his fast serve, Arthur spun his serves wide, favoring Jimmy's two-handed backhand. Instead of hitting his ground strokes with power, Ashe slowed things down and used more slice (which keeps the ball very low on a grass surface). The result was the biggest victory of Ashe's career. He beat Connors 6–1, 6–1, 5–7, 6–4.

Ashe never lost sight of his goal: winning the finals at Wimbledon. He wasn't attached to the way he was going to accomplish this. Rather than applying his strengths, he looked to see what Connors's weaknesses were and then attempted to exploit them. He was flexible, resourceful, and focused. Ashe later admitted that his unusual plan probably looked suicidal; however, the final results spoke for themselves.

The lesson we can draw from this is that just because we reach a certain level of proficiency, it doesn't always mean that we should apply the same techniques and strategies to every situation. Certain challenges will call for a shift in the way we think, behave, and approach our goals. There will be times when something different, out of the ordinary, or even opposite is called for. Isn't this how Muhammad Ali's defensive peek-a-boo approach beat George Foreman's offensive approach in Zaire? The 15 Second Principle can help us to become more creative and adaptive by reminding us to: stop, step outside our normal frame of reference, evaluate the options, change gears, and choose the most appropriate tactics. This, in turn, will enable us to become more versatile and adaptive performers.

◈SCUBA BREATHING ON LAND◈

I was blessed to have been introduced to scuba diving while visiting the Great Barrier Reef in Australia. Talk about getting spoiled early in one's scuba career. Whaw! The most valuable piece of scuba instruction I received was that regardless of what was happening or how much fear I was feeling, I should always *continue to breathe*. I could breathe slowly or quickly, gently or powerfully, with relaxation or nervousness, but I needed to continue to breathe. My instructor said that the only time I would really be in trouble was if I panicked and began to hold my breath. This breath-holding would set up a dangerous environment that could produce disastrous results.

This scuba advice can also be applied to areas of our life on land. A continuous breathing pattern can provide us with additional energy and serenity in every aspect of our lives. By continuously inhaling and exhaling, it is much easier to live in present time, rather than dwelling in the past or future. In addition, a gentle and continuous breath helps to quiet a chattering and frenetic mind. For some mysterious reason it is difficult to worry when you are breathing.

Unfortunately most of us just assume that because we are still alive, we must be breathing properly. This is not necessarily true. Some breathing patterns are healthier and more invigorating than others. Some will energize us; others can restrict and stifle us. How we breathe can have a profound effect on the quality of our lives.

The first step in building a more efficient breathing pattern is to become more aware of our current pattern. Most of the time, instead of a continuous scuba breath, our pattern is composed of a series of starts and stops. We are either holding our breath after we inhale or we are holding our breath after we exhale. Either way, the breath is being held for extended periods of time.

The second step is to begin using a continuous scuba breathing pattern more of the time. Your ultimate goal is to be breathing automatically in this scuba manner. This will be a lifelong challenge, so be gentle and patient with yourself. When I first began this continuous breathing approach, I would constantly catch myself holding my breath.

The third step is to increase the amount of air you take in with each inhalation. Rather than weak or shallow breaths, attempt to draw more air into your lungs.

The more comfortable and relaxed you are with a person, the more continuous and natural your breath will automatically become. In contrast, during uncomfortable, important, and emergency situations, you will tend to take shallow breaths and/or hold your breath. This is not ideal breathing because in potentially stressful situations, the body needs more relaxation and oxygen, not less. Shallow breathing or holding the breath are open invitations for tension, fear, and doubt to flourish.

Your goal is to create more of a natural and fluid breathing rhythm. While there are probably hundreds of different ways to breathe (as in meditation and yoga), my suggestion is to experiment with this simple and continuous breathing technique first. Ultimately, you want to select a pattern or create one that is easy to understand and enjoyable to exe-cute. Below are a few suggestions. Be sure to use these suggestions as guidelines rather than rules.

1. *Circular breathing.* Your mission in this scuba-type breathing is to have no beginning or end to your breathing. You may prefer to think of this as *connected* or *infinite* breathing. Just as a circle and infinity sign have no beginning or end, neither should your breath. (Olympic swimmers don't stop when they are doing laps in the pool; neither should you stop your breathing.)

2. Let your body work more during the inhalation and less during the exhalation. The inhalation should be pleasurable work while the exhalation should be pleasurable relaxation. Picture the waves of the ocean breaking and coming into shore. The waves have more power and energy coming in (inhaling) and less force and speed going back out to sea (exhaling).

3. *Continuous elevator breathing.* Imagine there is an elevator shaft inside of you. It begins at the base of your belly and spine. The shaft continues up through your neck and ends in your brain. Your goal is to draw air way up the shaft and into your brain. It's helpful to imagine that your lungs are in your head. Your mission is to fill your brain with oxygen and then to relax and let the carbon dioxide escape by itself. You want to work harder bringing air up the shaft than you do when releasing the air out of your mouth and nose. Because the breathing is continuous, the elevator will not be stopping at any floor. It will keep going from the basement, up to the penthouse, and then back down again. This is a great way to breathe for short periods of time when you need to quickly energize yourself.

4. *Continuous belly breathing.* Imagine your lungs have now been moved to your stomach. Your goal is to fill your stomach with air (inhale), and then to *let* the air escape out of your mouth and/or nose (exhale). If done correctly, your belly will expand when inhaling and recede when exhaling. This is a soothing and efficient way to breathe for long periods of time. It puts very little stress on your body.

5. The act of breathing can be extremely helpful when you are playing golf, tennis, or baseball. As you are swinging – before, during, and after contact with the ball – it is important to keep the body in a relaxed and trusting state. This can be done by gently exhaling (or inhaling) throughout the swinging motion. If exhaling, direct a gentle column of air directly toward the ball. This column should continue until after the moment of contact occurs with the ball. If you choose to inhale, imagine that your narrow and gentle column of air is now vacuuming the ball up. Both inhaling and exhaling actions will encourage you to live in present time (rather than worrying about the past or the future), remain more relaxed, and encourage your head to remain stationary until after the moment of contact has occurred. (This same method of breathing can be applied when attempting to catch a ball.)

6. Breathing can also be used when we are late for an appointment. The stress induced by being late often causes us to hold our breath or to breathe in a shallow fashion. Regardless of whether you are stuck in traffic or racing to complete a project or take an exam, remember to breathe.

7. Continuous breathing is also useful when you are talking to someone. If you ever find yourself becoming tense or self-conscious during a conversation, be aware that the first thing that will generally shut down is your breath. Once this occurs, it becomes very difficult to be relaxed and spontaneous. This is especially true when you are listening. By reminding yourself to keep inhaling and exhaling (slowly and gently), you will regain your relaxation, balance, and focus.

A word of caution is needed here. Be sure to ease into this new breathing pattern. New breathing techniques usually cause some initial light-headedness and dizziness. If this happens, don't panic. Just relax, sit down for a while, and stop using this new breathing pattern until the symptoms cease. Your body needs time to practice in order to become accustomed to this new breathing approach. Due to possible dizziness and initial highs, do not attempt to learn these breathing patterns while driving a car or operating a potentially dangerous piece of equipment. In addition, you want to guard against a self-induced state of hyperventilation. Your breathing need not be rapid and intense. Rather, it should be slow and gentle. I never heard of anyone dying from hyperventilation, but it does have a tendency to cause people to panic unnecessarily.

In closing, pay more attention to your breathing patterns. This is especially true in overly stressful situations. The more you understand the power and centering nature of the breath, the freer and more serene your life can become.

*The process of breathing lies at the center of every action
and reaction we make or have, and so by returning to it we
go to the core of the stress response ... When we breathe well,
we create the optimum conditions for health and well-being.*
                                                    —Donna Farhi,
                                  internationally known yoga instructor

◆ ALBERTO RIZZO'S DISCOVERY ◆

Many summers ago I visited friends on Long Island for the weekend. Staying with them was a fascinating man named Alberto
Rizzo. Alberto turned out to be an internationally known photo-
grapher who was currently based in New York City. I asked him
how many years he had been involved in photography before he
became recognized as an artist. Alberto's response amazed me.
He answered, "One year." His story is quite inspirational.

Alberto was always involved with the arts, specifically dance,
acting, and music. He pursued these professionally until he was
in his early forties. Then one day he picked up his wife's camera,
looked through the lens, and thought that shooting a roll of film
would be fun. The experience was so enjoyable that he shot
another roll and then another. This passionate process seduced
him into stopping everything else and devoting a year of his life
to photography. He described his commitment as "living with the
camera."

Alberto's challenge was to capture on film what his eye saw and
his heart felt. His goal was to give his audience the same emotional response that he experienced. In a sense, he immersed himself
in photography for a year in order to learn how to communicate
in an entirely new language called photography. In retrospect, he
believed it had taken him forty years to see and to feel and one
year to transfer those experiential abilities directly into a photo-
graph.

Until that moment, I always assumed that a professional pho-
tographer would have had to begin taking pictures at a very early
age. I also imagined that he probably would have built himself a
darkroom as a teenager, and that he would have taken dozens of

courses in every imaginable aspect of photography. To my surprise, Alberto's early photographic curriculum had been life, instead of an early passion and dedication to photography.

Whenever you feel like experimenting with a new hobby or profession, and the chatter of "But it's too late," comes barreling into your vulnerable mind, just remember Alberto Rizzo. It's rarely too late. Rather than being ruled by a disabling internal conversation, call upon The 15 Second Principle, and take one more mini-action in the direction of your special yet precious vision. Remember, with your passion and the wisdom of a master-teacher, many of those out-of-sight dreams can come into view.

LEVELS OF DISABILITY

Over the years, I have heard many stories about why people feel they're not talented enough to play tennis (or any other sport). Some reveal that they have terrible hand-to-eye coordination. Others claim that they don't have an aptitude for sports. Still others confess that they are too weak, heavy, awkward, or clumsy. Here is a story that just might place these "disabilities" into a different light.

Many years ago, I ran a wheelchair tennis program for Widney High School in Los Angeles. One day we received an invitation to fly two of our best wheelchair players to Little Rock, Arkansas, to participate in a wheelchair tennis demonstration. Augustine Luna and Fernando Guevara, two of our top players, accepted the invitation.

The purpose for a city to organize a wheelchair tennis event is usually twofold: First, they want to educate the general public about the world of wheelchair tennis. (In wheelchair tennis, the ball is allowed to bounce twice. All other rules remain the same.) Audiences are always amazed by this fantastic and very difficult sport. Second, they want to inspire and introduce tennis to other wheelchair-bound people. New potential players actually get a chance to participate in the sport. It is hoped that their experience will be so positive that they will be inspired to pursue wheelchair tennis.

To accomplish this orientation program, wheelchair tennis players usually volunteer their services and give a free introductory clinic to wheelchair-bound people. Fernando and Augustine were asked to join the teaching staff for this part of the program. As soon as the free clinic was announced, many new prospective players responded by wheeling their chairs onto the tennis court. The organizers were delighted by the response. A few minutes later, I realized that I had lost track of Augustine. After looking all around the arena, I finally spotted him in a back corner of one of the courts. While I couldn't quite make out what he was doing, it appeared that he was somehow preparing one of the new players for his first wheelchair tennis lesson. When I got closer, I couldn't believe my eyes. What I witnessed was Augustine strapping and securing a tennis racquet to the stump of a young man's upper right arm. Suddenly Augustine, a paraplegic, appeared to be quite able-bodied as he fastened a long leather strap around the remainder of this quadriplegic man's arm.

At that moment, I had a profound realization about the levels of our own disabilities. As bad as our disability might be, rest assured that there will always be someone, somewhere, whose afflictions will be worse. While some disabilities are obviously worse than others, we should never allow them to stop us from challenging ourselves and participating in life. Always remember that passion, patience, and dedication can overcome a massive deficiency of talent or aptitude. Just because we may not have a natural gift for something, it doesn't mean that we can't have a wonderful time learning and improving.

This Little Rock experience had a profound influence on my life. It made me understand that the only real crippling disabilities we have are our own limiting thoughts and belief systems. When we latch on to a handy problem and let it stop our passion or progress, only then have we created a personal handicap.

Anytime the thought comes up that you aren't smart or talented enough to pursue something that you are curious about, stop and apply The 15 Second Principle. Ask yourself if all of these doubts and fears are appropriate feelings for the current circumstances. More often than not, old beliefs and pictures are activating the uncomfortable sensations. Therefore, if you love it, pursue it in spite of the internal chatter and discomfort. Take one more mini-action, ask one more question, learn one more fact. Don't let fear or the unknown prevent you from being in motion. Life is too short and precious to let uncomfortable sensa-tions and dis-abilities prevent you from realizing your dreams.

Home Runs and Foul Tips:
Close Encounters on
Life's Playing Field

*Stories are medicine ... They have such power; they do
not require that we do, be, act anything – we need only
listen. The remedies for repair or reclamation of any lost
psychic drive are contained in stories.*
                                    —*Clarissa Pinkola Estes, Ph.D.*

Every now and then, as we pass through this world, things happen to us that are unusual and memorable. These unique
experiences can at times be enjoyable and at other times
embarrassing. Even when these indelible moments are uncomfortable, they can turn out to be educational and, in hindsight, even
funny. I have been blessed with many such personal encounters.
These experiences contain some of my most lasting life lessons.
Some of these personal stories are about how to perform; others
deal with how not to perform. I have included some of my less stellar moments because many of our greatest lessons come from our
most painful experiences.

Although several of these stories might appear to be those of a
foolish performer, they are of someone who, on a conscious level,
was always trying to do his best. I hope that after reading about
my experiences you will not need to make the same mistakes I
did. If I can save you a little time and prevent you from falling
into similar pitfalls, then my faux pas and missteps will have
helped to keep you on a more masterful path.

ASKING FOR A RAISE
AT WILLIAM MORRIS AGENCY

My initiation into the entertainment industry began many years ago at the William Morris Agency in New York. At that time it was the oldest, largest, and most powerful theatrical booking agency in the world. At one time or another, just about every major performer, producer, writer, and director passed through William Morris's doors.

I started by working in their grueling agent-training program. The company's policy was to begin the trainees from the ground up. Now, when I say *ground,* I mean *ground.* First, you had to get through an intense interview session. If you were successful, you would begin working in the mail room. This would entail becoming a well-dressed (suit and tie) "go-fer." You'd run errands, Xerox, sort the mail, and deliver it to the agents' secretaries in supermarket shopping carts. This trainee tradition had gone on for decades.* The company believed that the mail room experience provided the best overview of how the entire organization operated. Depending on luck, timing, and your personality, the mail room phase lasted from one month to two years.

Once you were promoted, you would become a secretary to one of the agents. (While I was in the mail room they sent me to secretarial night school to learn typing and shorthand.) If you were lucky enough not to be fired for being a terrible secretary, this phase usually lasted from one to three years. The next promotion would be to junior agent, and finally, to agent.

Let's talk agent trainee salary. Because so many people wanted to get into show biz, the company got away with paying minimum wage. If you had a bachelor's degree they would normally start you out at seventy-five dollars a week. Because I was finishing up my M.B.A. degree they stretched and started me out at ninety

---

* Mike Ovitz, David Geffen, and Barry Diller, three entertainment industry giants, started their show business careers in the WMA agent-training program. As of the publication date of this book, the agency still runs an agent training program.

dollars a week (that's gross, very gross, not net). Wayne, who came in the week after I did, and who had just received his law degree, was also awarded the additional fifteen-dollar-a-week bonus.

If the agency could have legally gotten away with it, they would have charged us for the opportunity to work there. The way they looked at it, there was no university on earth where you could make these kinds of contacts and learn the business. They believed (and rightly so) that WMA was the Harvard of the entertainment industry. To them, my ninety-dollar salary was a generous scholarship rather than a meager salary.

The pervading tone and attitude of the agency resembled a well-to-do fraternity. The agents were the brothers (and a few sisters), and the trainees were the lowlife, powerless pledges. To say that we were always walking on thin ice is an understatement. If two WMA brothers in the house didn't like a pledge and they made their unhappiness known to management, the pledge could easily be blackballed (fired).

The head of administration and operations was Lee Stevens, who later went on to become the president of the agency. For anything major (promotions, pay raises, firings), you would have to travel up to the thirty-third floor and see the omnipotent Mr. Stevens. The trainees never looked forward to this experience because none of us had any rapport or relationship with this very tall, serious, and seemingly distant man. Whenever you'd pass him in the narrow hallways, he would never make eye contact with you. Instead he would always look straight ahead, making you feel like Casper the Ghost. Because he was the designated hatchet man in the company, and there was a lot of chopping to do, he probably didn't want to get too friendly with any trainees that he might have to fire. The law of the mail room was never, ever get yourself on the wrong side of this man. If you did, it would be next to impossible to brother up and become an agent.

After working at the agency for two years (I was now a secretary making all of $120 a week), I reluctantly decided that it was time to have my first meeting with Mr. Stevens. I felt that I desperately needed a raise. I sent him an interoffice memo requesting a pow-wow.

A week later, I got a call from Phyllis, his secretary. She informed me that he was very busy and asked if I still wanted to see him about my raise. I said I did. In a humorous yet concerned voice she asked, "Are you sure?"

"I think I'm sure" was my reply. She then told me to come by at three o'clock and to be prepared. She ended the conversation with, "If he opens his desk drawer, you are in a lot of trouble. Good luck."

At three o'clock sharp, I went to the very quiet and austere executive wing of the thirty-third floor and checked in with Phyllis. She buzzed him, and in no time I was in his office. Without looking directly at me, he motioned for me to sit down on a straight-back chair directly across from his desk. Just as I sat down, he threw these intense, laser-beam eyes in my direction. His first words were: "What did you want to talk to me about?" Feeling very uncomfortable, I blurted out, "Money." He retaliated with one word: "Why?"

"Excuse me?" I said.

"Why?" he repeated. I couldn't believe my ears. I knew, however, that I had better fill the silence with something. "I need a raise – I need a raise because. . .because I'm supposed to know what's going on in the entertainment industry, yet I can't even afford to go to a movie or, God forbid, see a play. I need a raise to stay better informed." Being quite impressed by my own survival babble, I rested my case.

For a few seconds, he was silent. He then proceeded in almost a religious fashion to place his fingers gently on the handle of that infamous desk drawer that I was warned about. He then slowly opened it and removed a small piece of paper. I was relieved it wasn't a gun. "How much are you making now?" he asked.

"One hundred and twenty a week," I responded.

He winced as though I was ripping the company off big time. He then informed me that he was holding the stub of *his* weekly salary check from his secretarial trainee days at WMA. He turned the stub around so that I could read it. The stub started with a gross of thirty-five dollars and then worked its way down with city, state, and federal deductions. I now understood why Phyllis had wished me luck.

His large office began to feel extremely hot, humid, and small. "You work for Sandy Littman, don't you?" he said. "Yes," I responded. "Well," he said, "Sandy probably knows more people in the entertainment industry than anyone else in the agency. If you can't learn from Sandy how to get some screening passes and complimentary Broadway tickets, then you really shouldn't be working at this agency." By this time, I felt like I was in a steam room. "Now, do you or don't you think you can learn this skill from Sandy?" he asked.

"Yes, I think so, sir" was my meek reply.

He smiled and said, "Good."

I couldn't believe it. Within two minutes, the man had disarmed me, thrown me to the ground, and put his knee against my throat. What on earth could I possibly say that would turn this conversation around? I needed a verbal miracle. I waited for a few seconds and then found myself genuinely thanking him for helping me with a serious situation. After all, I had come to him with an entertainment problem and he had given me a solution – complimentary tickets. He seemed very pleased that I had seen the light. I then said, "Before I leave, sir, perhaps you could help me out by solving just one more problem?" He seemed surprised and in a softer and more helpful tone responded, "I'll try." I waited a second and then asked, "Would you also know where I could get some free food?"

There was a second of silence before uncontrollable screams of laughter burst out of his mouth. This volcanic eruption brought Phyllis rushing into his office. I guess she thought he was being attacked. He immediately motioned her to leave the room, much the same way a prize fighter would wave away his trainer after being hit by a great punch. With tears in his eyes, he looked like a man who knew he had been beaten at his own game. He looked at me, smiled, and said, "Get out of here. I'll see what I can do."

The next week, a farewell retirement banquet was being thrown for an ex-boss of mine, Ben Griefer. Because I had been his secretary, I was invited to attend this very exclusive executive luncheon. Being the most junior member of this entire gathering (by many years and even more power tiers), I felt extremely conspicuous and out of place. Legendary WMA figures such as Nat

Lefkowitz (president) and Howard Hausman (head of the motion picture department) were present. As I sat among the East Coast ruling class of the agency, I suddenly felt the presence of someone standing right behind me. I looked straight up, pointing my nose and chin up toward the ceiling, to discover Mr. Stevens's face staring straight down at me. He was smirking as he said, "Per our conversation, I thought you might need this." Immediately, a huge hard dinner roll came crashing down onto my plate, almost cracking it. He then added, "Now, I never want to hear that I've never given you anything." He then smiled and walked back to his seat. At long last one of my dreams had come true. I had finally been acknowledged in public by Mr. Stevens. Along with the roll came a fifteen-dollar-a-week raise.

If there is a moral to this story, it is that when all else fails, try humor. If used properly, humor can act as a wonderful mood interrupter. It can sometimes salvage the most serious and hopeless situations. Because the best humor contains love and at times a self-deprecating spirit, it has the power to disarm even the most brilliant negotiator. Bear in mind, however, that if used incorrectly, it can cause embarrassment, pain, and damage. That's why appropriateness and timing are so crucial to a comedic approach. When dealing with humor, there's a very fine line separating success and disaster.

By thanking Mr. Stevens for his help and advice, I also removed myself from an adversarial role. Rather than barreling forward, digging in, or pleading my case further, I immediately dropped my position and joined his point of view. Applying The 15 Second Principle by waiting a beat and then thanking him, I created the illusion that we were on the same harmonic team. This enabled me to tiptoe up from the rear and surprise him.

Due to the tenuous nature of comedy, being prepared is still the best name of the negotiating game. Before entering a meeting or giving a presentation, rehearse all worst-case scenarios. (This is something I obviously neglected to do.) You want to be relaxed and ready for any questions or curves that might be thrown your way. Let preparation be your ship and comedy be your life raft.

◢IT'S THE WHAT, NOT THE HOW◣

On Tuesday, January 9, 1996, I read a notice in the *Hollywood Reporter* that stated that Miramax Pictures was celebrating the success of their picture *The Postman* (*Il Postino*) with a celebrity reception. The event would honor the poetry of Pablo Neruda. It was to be held at the Wolfgang Puck Cafe on Sunset Boulevard in Los Angeles, and would begin at 7:00 P.M. Following a cocktail party, many celebrities would read their favorite Neruda poem.

Because I loved the movie *Il Postino* and appreciate the poetry of Neruda, I decided to call the restaurant to find out if there were any tickets still available. I was told that the event was by invitation only and that you had to be a guest of Miramax. Although this news was quite bleak, I was so excited about the event that I decided not to give up hope. I figured that perhaps I would bump into a show business friend who might have an extra ticket.

Whenever I don't have an invitation or ticket for a function that I want to attend, I attempt to put myself through a successful imaginary scenario before I go. The more convincing and vivid I can make the imaginary journey, by using all of my senses, the better. On a visceral level, my body and mind should prematurely *experience* the event. Psychologists tell us that the more believable our imagination can make something, the more difficult it is for our brain to distinguish a graphic wish from a reality. So, once we internally can make the imaginary scenario believable and successful, it becomes much easier to go out and actually produce a real, successful result. Now back to our story.

After experiencing a successful Mission Possible at home, I set out for the cafe. When I arrived at around 7:00 P.M., I was impressed by the length of the red carpet leading to the entrance and by the number of paparazzi waiting to pounce on the celebrities once they left the restaurant. At the same time, I was unimpressed by two realities. First, it was turning into a cold evening. Second, the security at the restaurant was very tight. Refusing to succumb to the hopeless themes beginning to play inside my head, I used The 15 Second Principle to reexperience my successful Mission Possible. I then zippered my jacket and walked to the back of the short line adjacent to the restaurant.

At some point I got the courage to ask someone what the line I was waiting in was for. It turned out to be a line filled with angry people who were holding invitations. Apparently, the event was overinvited. Becoming colder by the minute, I still was determined not to let the circumstances get the best of me.

After patiently waiting in line for several more minutes, miraculously I saw an old friend walk out of the restaurant and begin to look around. Feeling quite powerless, I yelled, "Anita, help." Anita came over and tried to assist me. As it turns out, she had contacts at Miramax. Within five minutes, she reappeared with an invitation. The bad news, however, was that I was still stuck in the overinvited line and my name was still not on any official RSVP list.

The longer I waited, the colder and angrier everyone became. Finally, after my body had become chilled to the bone, I realized that the event would be over before this line was going to move. This feeling became so strong that I abandoned the line – but not my vision. After mulling around for a while, one of my grandfather's brilliantly trite expressions crossed my mind: "If at first you don't succeed, try, try again."

"But I have tried and tried again," I whimpered back to the ghost of his wisdom.

"You have tried everyone's way but your own" was the answer I received.

Having remnants of childhood dyslexia, I knew exactly what this meant. My way was usually backwards, upside down, and opposite from everyone else's. I immediately thought, *If there is a front entrance, there must be a back entrance.* After all, Wolfgang Puck was too cool a guy to have his garbage dragged out the front door. With a shivering body, I walked to the back of the building and attempted to open a door that I thought might be part of the restaurant. Bingo, it was the restaurant. The only problem was that it was the kitchen, and dozens of helpers and many chefs were running around as if their lives were at stake. I thought, *Do I have the nerve to walk arrogantly through the kitchen as though I were Wolfgang Puck's half-brother?* When I answered "No," I passed on the Puck part and closed the door.

My next thought was, *Is this the only back door in town?* As I continued snooping around, two people, who seemed to know where they were going, quickly walked past me. I decided to follow them. They opened and walked through one set of doors. Then, instead of walking down a flight of stairs, they moved forward and knocked three times on a metal door. The door opened, and they immediately entered and disappeared. Being a cold and desperate explorer, I seized the moment by leaping forward and grabbing the door just before it closed. Even though I had no idea of what establishment I was entering, I entered with the confidence of Wolfgang Puck's half-cousin.

The room I entered was hot, crowded, and dark. As soon as my eyes adjusted to the darkness, I was shocked to discover where I was. Not only was I in the Wolfgang Puck Cafe, but I was in the private celebrity section. What I had entered was the makeshift backstage waiting area for the poetry readers. Within a fifteen-foot radius of me were the likes of Jacqueline Bisset, James Woods, Maximillian Schell, Patrick Stewart, Rod Steiger, Jennifer Tilly, Melissa Etheridge, and Sally Kellerman. Because some of these celebrities were old tennis friends, I felt quite comfortable chatting with some of them. I was also delighted to discover that I was in a perfect location to hear everyone's favorite Neruda poem. Afterward, Anita invited me back to her table where I was treated to some pasta and wine.

I learned many lessons from this experience, but the most important one deals with a powerful metaphysical principle that has served me very well over the years. I call it, "It's the what, not the how!" Once you can get clear on exactly *what* you want, and stay committed and recommitted to the what, the universe will help you create more of the hows. While I didn't know how I was going to get into Wolfgang Puck's, I definitely knew the what – that I wanted to attend the reception.

Unfortunately many people get stuck in the hows. Unless they know exactly how to do something or until they know how something is going to turn out, they are hesitant to begin a project. However, the more precise and focused we can become on our whats, the luckier we somehow become. More often than not our clarity of purpose, focused attention, and willingness to live in present time create a magnetic field that attracts helpful people to us and attracts us to serendipitous circumstances.

It is useful to imagine that each of us is connected to an infinite computer that is capable of helping us to materialize many things. What the computer requires, however, is a very specific request to be spelled out and programmed in. You and the computer work as a team. As you work in the tangible world, the computer works in the intangible world.

With regards to programming the computer, if you are a commitment-phobic person, relax. This commitment is not a "till death do us part" kind of a relationship. The computer doesn't care if at some point you change your mind and choose another goal. This computer is similar to an elevator. Just entering the car is not enough. The elevator needs to be told to which floor you want it to go. Your job is to pick a *specific* floor and push the exact button. It will do the rest. You don't need to know how the elevator works. When you arrive at your desired floor, you are once again free to push a different button.

Director Anthony Minghella, whose movie *The English Patient* won nine Academy Awards, describes one of the realities of directing a scene in a movie as, "If you do not know what you want, absolutely nothing happens." Because each of us has the potential to become the director and star of our own movie called *My Life,* why not get a little daring by adding some generous and specific whats to our personal screenplay? Then all we will have to do is to keep honing our "how-to" skills. One of the most important how-to skills is knowing what questions to ask and whom to ask. By presenting yourself as an inquisitive beginner and not as a confident expert, many knowledgeable people will go out of their way to help you.

Anytime you find yourself mentally, physically, or emotionally wavering, take *one more action*. Although it might not always appear to be an efficient one, take it anyway. This is where The 15 Second Principle can spring into action. Even minuscule actions have the power to shift your mood and change your perceptions. Regardless of how you feel, be courageous enough to make that call, or begin writing that letter. Your commitment is to your commitment, not to your emotions or beliefs.* Once your system understands that your moods, fears, and obstacles will no longer determine when and where you take actions, you will begin to take back control of your life.

> *You have to know what you want to get, but when you know that, let it take you.*
>
> *And if it seems to take you off the track, Don't hold back, because perhaps that is instinctively where you want to be.*
>
> *And if you hold back and try to be always where you have been before, you will go dry.*
>
> —*Gertrude Stein*

◆ IS PRACTICING REALLY NECESSARY ◆

Many years ago, while living in New York, I received a call from my friend Dennis Elliott. Dennis is a very gifted trombonist and at seventeen was the youngest member ever to be accepted into Radio City Music Hall's orchestra. He told me that a National Guard marching band was holding auditions, and suggested that I grab my flute and saxophone and meet him down at a Brooklyn armory. I tried explaining to him that I hadn't been practicing much, and that my sight-reading skills were stale, but he reminded me that the Vietnam War was still on and that carrying a flute was probably safer than carrying a rifle. He also informed me that the National Guard had just dropped its policy of shooting musicians who had terrible auditions.

When we arrived at the armory, I was told that the band was in desperate need of a flute player. In fact, at that moment there weren't any flutists in the entire band. Although my audition was less than brilliant, the bandmaster reluctantly accepted me and gave me a quick limp handshake. Dennis, on the other hand, was welcomed with a huge hug and a salute.

---

* I am assuming that you are not in an extremely fragile emotional or physical state. If you feel you are about to have a nervous breakdown or drop from exhaustion, do not push yourself by executing any more mini-actions.

Within a few minutes, I was handed a full marching uniform and told to report in three days for the St. Patrick's Day Parade. When I asked whether I could try on the uniform, I was told no. Mine was the last uniform in the box, and I had to make do with whatever I was given. I next asked if I could see the music that we were going to be playing. Once again I was told no. It was supposedly locked up in some old metal cabinet.

When I got home, the first thing I did was to put the uniform on. After looking in the mirror, I didn't know whether to laugh or cry. As I found out later, the uniform had previously belonged to a five-foot, two-inch, rotund trumpet player who weighed in at 200 pounds. I was five-nine and tipped the scales at 140. I knew I was going to look more like a walking scarecrow and less like a member of a National Guard band.

When I woke up on March seventeenth, the temperature was in the low thirties. *Oh boy*, I thought, *this is going to be one challenging day*. I put my uniform into a small suitcase (I wouldn't dare wear it on the subway), threw in some long underwear, and headed on down to the Lower East Side of Manhattan.

When I arrived at the downtown armory, I sensed that I was in the midst of a very professional group of musicians. I immediately noticed Lou Soloff, one of the hottest trumpet players in the country. (He played lead trumpet for Blood, Sweat & Tears.) *Oh my God*, I thought, *what in the world am I doing here?*

After I'd put on my beautiful uniform, a sergeant came over and handed me a very small musical case. When I asked what it was, he said, "A piccolo." When I asked what I should do with it, he said, "Play it." When I asked when I should play it, he said, "Today." I gasped. When I explained that I hadn't touched a piccolo in twelve years, he looked quite uninterested. "Soldier, put your flute away and let's get marching" was his militaristic response.

I was next given a pair of white gloves, a small book of music, and a portable music holder called a lyre. Because the piccolo is so small, a music holder can't be attached directly to the instrument. Instead, the music is fastened to a lyre, which resembles a huge wooden spoon. You stick the wider section of the wooden lyre under your armpit and you attach the music to the narrower end. The more you press your arm and elbow in, the more secure the lyre becomes.

As we filed outdoors, I was delighted that I had put on my long underwear. It was cold, damp, and dreary. When we got into formation, I started to realize just how much trouble I was in. First, it was freezing, and playing most metal instruments in the cold is very difficult. Second, I had never simultaneously marched and played music before. Third, I didn't have time to look at the music. Fourth, the lyre didn't like staying under my armpit. Fifth, I had never played music while wearing gloves. Sixth, I was still very self-conscious about my scarecrow uniform and loose-fitting hat. Needless to say, I had my work cut out for me.

The band was positioned behind approximately fifty policemen on horseback. Behind us was a cast of thousands. As soon as the horses began to move, we were off and marching up Park Avenue. I was delighted to discover that we didn't have to play music at first. The drummers supplied a very energizing, crisp beat. This gave me a chance to get the rust out of my marching legs. "Left, right, left, right, left, right." For the first five minutes, because I didn't have to play, I must admit that I was having a wonderful time. My most challenging task was hopping over and weaving around the mounds of steaming Manhattan muffins that the horses were depositing on Park Avenue. The farther north we marched, the deeper and more enthusiastic the crowds became.

The next thing I knew, the bandmaster turned his head around and yelled, "Number twenty-eight." I turned to that number, prayed, and played. To my surprise, some correct notes were actually coming out of the frozen piccolo. The more I played, the more comfortable I became. My playing and marching were slowly but surely improving. I kept thinking how brilliant the human body really was. After the first song, the drummers once again took over. As we turned left on Twenty-third Street and headed west, I noticed how much thicker the crowds were becoming.

After playing one more easy march, the bandmaster yelled, "Twenty-four!" I flipped the music to page twenty-four just to discover my most horrendous nightmare staring me in the face. It was "Stars and Stripes Forever." This piece of music contains the killer of killer piccolo solos. *He's got to be kidding*, I thought. In my prime piccolo days, I never came close to cutting this solo. I knew that the odds of getting through it now were virtually impossible. I tried getting the bandmaster's attention, but he had already turned his proud and uplifted head away from us. I secured the lyre under my armpit, pulled my hat down, adjusted my gloves, prayed to the heavens, and began to play.

To my delight, I started to perform fairly well. At least I was playing most of the notes. Then came the musical challenge of my life: the solo. Most of the band, being very curious about my skills, got extremely quiet. As I began, I couldn't believe my ears or fingers. It was as though the ghost of a proficient piccolo player had invaded my body. While some wrong notes did come out, I was managing to play a lot of the correct ones. After a few seconds into this miraculous solo, I must admit that my next thought was, *Wouldn't it be great if we were being televised.*

Then suddenly, in the middle of this amazing solo, my entire body hit something hard, big, and stationary. My nose felt like it had gone up to meet my brain as my piccolo, music, lyre, and hat fell to the ground. I couldn't see a thing. With blurry stars in my eyes, I attempted to regain my balance by touching the thing that was directly in front of me. It was solid, had leather and fur. As my vision improved I looked up and discovered a policeman's leather boot and a huge furry horse. The policeman seemed quite amused as he smiled, pointed, and said, "The band went thataway." I quickly turned and followed his finger. What I discovered was that the band had made a sharp right turn and had gone directly up Fifth Avenue. I, on the other hand, following the beat of another drummer, kept marching straight across Fifth Avenue until I merged with a policeman on a stationary horse.

As the crowds behind the barricades laughed and jeered at me, I bent down and quickly picked up my piccolo, music, hat, and lyre. I then began a panicked sprint up Fifth Avenue. Suddenly, and out of nowhere, a military jeep pulled up alongside me. There was a major sitting in the shotgun seat. By the red look on his face and the blue veins popping out of his neck, I knew that this was not a happy soldier. He then screamed, "If you can't play and march at the same time, then for God's sake *stop playing* and just march." Seeing as he was about to hemorrhage, and not wanting his death on my conscience or fresh record, I decided just to march and fake playing the slightly bent piccolo. Thanks to the major's request, I didn't play one wrong note for the remainder of the day!

Although the bandmaster never discussed this incident with me, I'm sure he knew what had happened because we never again performed or practiced "Stars and Stripes Forever." The other members of the band weren't as kind as the bandmaster. They attempted to start a piccolo scholarship fund for me.

One of the lessons here is to stop and apply The 15 Second Principle by thinking of worst-case scenarios *before* they occur. If the worst-case scenario looks pretty bleak, we should take some precautionary actions to prevent it. We need to protect ourselves and our own well-being. Rather than assuming that others will be looking out for us, we must take responsibility and look out for ourselves. As they say in the army, C.Y.A. (cover your ass). Because I was intimidated by my first day in the National Guard, I neglected to ask the right questions and make some stronger artistic requests. Had I initially asked what instrument I was going to play, and had I demanded (or pleaded) to take the music home with me, this horrendous experience may never have happened. So, to answer the question in the title of this piece, "Is practicing really necessary?" The answer is unequivocally yes!

A "FANTASTICK" AUDITION

The Fantasticks is the longest-running play in the history of New York City. Periodically, they hold replacement auditions. Many years ago I received a call from my acting buddy, Terry Deck, informing me that they were once again auditioning actors. I promptly mailed my picture and résumé to the producers. Within a week, I miraculously received a call from the production office informing me that they wanted me to come in and read for the play.

When I called to confirm my appointment, I was told that I'd be auditioning for the part of Henry, the Old Actor. Seeing as I was twenty-nine, and looking more like nineteen, I found this casting choice very strange. When I suggested to the stage manager that I really should be auditioning for one of the younger roles, she replied, "Well, it's obvious that the producer and director think otherwise." Seeing as I was getting nowhere and knowing that these types of auditions were very difficult to get, I did not insist; I graciously accepted my appointment.

The next day around eleven o'clock, I began dressing for this challenging part. Picking the right clothing to make me look old was not an easy task. I finally settled on a baggy, ill-fitting three-piece suit. (A hand-me-down from a taller, wider, and richer friend.) After checking myself out in the mirror, I still looked decades too young. What was a youthful man to do? I went to my closet and took down a small box that contained acting makeup from some of my previous shows. While rummaging through the box, I found a can of white hair spray and immediately emptied half of it onto my long, curly, brown hair.

Next, I took a white grease stick and whitened my bushy mustache, sideburns, and eyebrows. I then threw on a pair of Benjamin Franklin–type eyeglasses. By this time, the years were flying by; I could barely recognize myself. There was only one problem. I had put on so much hair spray that it made my hair extremely hard and brittle. Everytime I touched my head, I was afraid that chunks of hair would break off.

I left my apartment around noon and began walking through the streets of Greenwich Village. The sun was blazing, and by the way people were staring at me, I figured that the sunlight must have been be ricocheting off my white hair in a strange way. Thinking that I might become less conspicuous by walking like an older man, I started getting more into character. Much to my dismay, even more people now began to stare.

When I finally entered the Sullivan Street Playhouse, I couldn't believe my eyes. There, sitting in the lobby, was a circle of at least twenty authentically old actors. And each one was older than the next. I looked like the youngest man by at least forty years. As I entered, all of these golden eyes turned and looked at me in dismay. Had Halloween arrived early? One ancient actor gave me a long hostile glare that I translated to mean: "I can't go up for the part of a young man, so why should you be allowed to go up for the part of an old man?" Sitting with my contemporaries and waiting for my turn was far from fun. I was greatly relieved when my name was finally called.

I stood up and, staying in character, walked into the theater as Old Henry. I knew I was in trouble, however, when the producer and director also looked at me in horror and dismay. Their eyes opened wide while their jaws dropped several inches. Then the producer asked, "Can we help you?"

I answered, "Yes, you can, sonny. I'm here to audition."

"You are," they responded. "For which part?"

"For the part of Old Henry," I said. They both looked at me like I was out of my mind. I then broke character and explained my confusion about being asked to audition for the older role. When they realized that they had made an error, apologies began to flow from their mouths. They were so embarrassed about their mistake and so impressed by the level of my creative preparation that they asked me if I wanted to stay and audition for the part. In an old man's voice I responded, "I sure do, young man."

This audition turned out to be the longest one I ever had. These guys kept giving me different scenes to read. They would then stop and direct me within each scene. The craziest thing was that the longer they worked with me, the more interested they seemed to become. I couldn't understand why they were spending so much time with a plastic rose when they had twenty blossoming rose bushes in the lobby.

Finally, the director said, "We'll call you tonight, either way." Now, you need to know that no one had ever said that to me after an audition. Instead, they would just thank me and let me leave. I thanked both of them and walked back to my apartment in a very pleasant old mood. It was wonderful to know that I was being considered for a part that my grandfather could also be up for.

Sure enough, later that evening, the director called me. He proceeded to give me the entire story in just one sentence. What he said was, "Thanks for a great audition, but we decided to go in another direction." What a way to turn someone down who showed up forty years too early. We decided to go in another direction. Yeah, like we decided to go in the real direction – an actual older man with gray hair and a naturally slow gate. What a creative concept. Seeing as I had forty more years to prepare for that "other direction," I took the news very well.

I learned two things from the *Fantasticks* audition. First, if your intuition tells you that something is wrong, trust the feeling. In hindsight, I should have applied The 15 Second Principle by politely insisting that the stage manager at least double-check with the director. Second, that you can make the best out of a bleak situation. Rather than turning down the audition over the phone, or walking out of the theater, I stayed and worked on my craft. And in the process of auditioning, I truly believe that I did get a little closer to winning the premature aging lottery.

◆ AUTHENTICITY IS THE NAME OF THE GAME ◆

Before my book *Ultimate Tennis* was published, I tried to find people to endorse it. I knew that to increase its chances of success, I needed the support of tennis celebrities who were much better known than I was. When I read that the La Quinta Hotel near Palm Springs was holding a tennis tournament, I decided to drive down to see if I could meet and interest some professional players in my dream project.

At La Quinta, I bumped into Hans, an old tennis buddy of mine. Hans gave me the good news that Stan Smith was playing in the tournament. Stan was a world champion, and is still one of the most respected men in tennis today. He won many major singles and doubles titles, including Wimbledon and the U.S. Open. Since Hans knew about my book and had a personal relationship with Stan, I asked him if he would mind introducing me to him. Hans declined, stating that although Stan was a very generous person, his policy was never to endorse anyone else's products. At this point I knew I was on my own.

La Quinta was always a wonderful tournament because you were able to see the greatest players on the planet at very close range. If you were persistent enough, you could usually say hello to any of them. At some point during the day, I spotted Stan talking to a few people. He was standing on the top of a small hill.

After he completed his conversation, I approached by walking up the incline. As I got closer, Stan kept getting taller. By the time I arrived, this six-foot, six-inch man appeared to be a giant. To look into his eyes, I had to stretch my neck and tilt my head way back. At this point, my Adam's apple was sticking out a mile. I felt like a vulnerable and meek four-year-old looking up at a huge sequoia. *Surely this is no way to begin a powerful sales pitch*, I thought.

To ease my awkwardness, Stan broke the ice by asking me what brought me to the tournament. While I thought about saying something very confident, grand, and positive about my tennis book, I just couldn't muster the courage to get behind that type of delivery. Out of sheer desperation, remaining in this power-less, defenseless, and childlike mode, I looked straight up at him and, with a weak and yet sincere voice, I spoke my truth: "Mr. Smith, I'm here to create a miracle."

Instantaneously, he became a gentle giant who seemed to be melting before my very eyes. He was quite interested in hearing what my miracle was all about. The more I told him about my book, the more he saw how passionate I was about this project. In addition, the more I described my mission, the more he understood how committed I was to helping people improve their tennis games. After talking to him for several minutes he asked me to meet him in the hotel's lounge after he completed his doubles match with Bob Lutz.

True to his word, he showed up soon after his match ended. He spent well over an hour looking through photocopied pages and pictures. Afterward, he asked whether I could meet him again the following morning. At the end of the second meeting, he requested that I send the entire manuscript to his home on Hilton Head Island, where he intended to finish looking it over. After receiving the book, reading it, and making some very helpful editorial suggestions, he miraculously agreed to endorse it. His endorsement made a huge difference in legitimizing my book. It also helped me to receive endorsements from Billie Jean King, Walter Cronkite, James Coburn, and Bruce Jenner.

I believe I was successful with Stan because I surrendered to the "powerless" reality of the moment. When he asked me what brought me to the tournament, I remained in a vulnerable and authentic state and spoke my truth. Instead of trying to disguise the fact that I felt small and insecure, I used my childlike meekness to my advantage. By riding this "powerless wave" in the direction it was already going and by not denying or changing my feelings, I became very persuasive and powerful. Going with the flow and being authentic enabled me to create a "miracle."

Another example of authenticity occurred many years ago while I was in basic training at Fort Dix, New Jersey. Our demanding drill instructor, Sergeant Hernandez, kept riding and screaming at poor Private Wilson. Whenever Wilson would manhandle his weapon (which was often), Hernandez would attack him with a barrage of verbal artillery. This abuse continued for days. Finally, Wilson became so nervous that he accidentally dropped his rifle right in front of Hernandez. The sergeant went ballistic. Putting his face into Wilson's, he screamed, "Why did you drop your rifle?" Wilson, looking more like a wounded dog than a soldier, responded, "I'm an idiot, Sergeant. It was a very stupid thing to do." Wilson then began to cry. Hernandez, seeing the private's distress, suddenly transformed into a tender, loving parent. He assured Wilson that it was not, in fact, a stupid thing to do and that it could happen to anyone. He put his hands on Wilson's shoulders and gave him a long pep talk. From that day forward, Wilson could do no wrong.

We need to trust that, most of the time, our real emotional state is more endearing than a false or superimposed one. Rather than covering up, it's better to be open and real. More often than not, our current emotions, if used appropriately, can be a powerful and persuasive sales tool.

This is also true in affairs of the heart. If you are attracted to someone but are scared and can't think of the appropriate line, do the following: Walk up to him or her, shaking legs and all, and say, "Hi. I'm a little nervous, but I thought I'd risk coming over to say hello." See what happens. You might be pleasantly surprised. It will certainly bring you more success than, "Hey, want to come up and see my etchings?" Fear and vulnerability, when used appropriately, can be powerful sales tools. The trick here is to be comfortable and playful with your insecurity. Once you can have fun creating a truthful environment, people may feel safe enough to let down some of their defenses. When this occurs, you will stand a much better chance of developing an empathetic relationship with them.

You are at your best when your thoughts, words, and actions are fully integrated and congruent. The cosmic joke is that the real and susceptible you is usually much more appealing than the you that you wish you were. If someone is going to reject you, at least let them reject the most truthful, vulnerable, and honest you.

What we are talking about is the ability to have our outsides match our insides. This will require an enormous amount of strength and courage. This is because all of our dysfunctional survival mechanisms will cry out for us to be anything but integrated. To prevent this from happening, apply The 15 Second Principle by daring to be authentic whenever you catch yourself being inauthentic. Trust that authenticity can set you free and that self-revelation can be very contagious. Remember, if you are never willing to risk by playing the part of the sincere fool, your fear will usually rule.

◆DIRECTIONS AND DETOURS◆

After leaving the William Morris Agency, I decided to study acting and to pursue comedy. The problem was that too many acting teachers were laughing at my acting and too many audiences in comedy clubs were crying at my humor. To improve my acting, I auditioned for as many parts as I could. That's what motivated me to audition for a small part in an off-Broadway play called *Barroca*. It was a Puerto Rican musical. I didn't feel or look Puerto Rican, but I needed the auditioning practice. Although I tried out for a small part, much to my delight and dismay, I got offered a very large part – the male lead!

The problem was that I didn't have any solid acting technique that I felt comfortable using. What I did have were the voices and theories of many acting teachers simultaneously floating around my brain. I also had never sung professionally. To say that I was a nervous wreck after accepting this part is an understatement.

There were so many lines to memorize, so many songs to sing, and so many emotions to have. While the director worked with me for hours at a time, I never quite understood what he wanted me to do or how I was going to fill the character's shoes.

While I knew that it was an incredible opportunity, and I was working with a very professional cast, I was putting so much pressure on myself that I was hoping that some catastrophe would come along and save me. Perhaps a broken leg, or a fire in the theater. Well, fortunately or unfortunately, God had other plans. When opening night arrived I was still healthy and the theater was still safe.

With my parents, friends, and relatives in the audience, I went out on the big stage and did the impossible. I actually got through the entire play without fainting, forgetting a line, or hitting a wrong note. During the celebratory cast party, I felt like a relieved war hero who was thrilled at still being alive.

The reality of being a lead in a play didn't hit me until the following morning. I woke up in a cold sweat. I realized that I had to go out there again that very evening and slay the dragons and do the impossible again. I stayed in all day and rested up. Very late in the afternoon, the phone rang. It was a cast member telling me that the play had gotten a great review in the *New York Post*. I was ecstatic.

On my way to the theater, I walked up Sixth Avenue to my local newsstand and shared my excitement with Eddie the newsstand guy. I asked him if he had twenty copies of the *Post*, and if so, to wrap them up for me. I figured I'd give them out as gifts to the cast. He wrapped up nineteen and gave me one to read.

After lugging the papers for two blocks, my excitement and curiosity got the best of me. Even though it had begun to snow, I just couldn't wait until I got into the subway. I had to take a peek at the review. I found a streetlight, put the heavy bundle down, and opened the *Post*. After flipping through many pages I came across a huge, full-page spread on the play. Pictures and all. They had given us great exposure because it was the first Puerto Rican musical ever to play in Manhattan. I started reading the paper, and it was apparent that the reviewer really liked the show. At first I had difficulty finding my name, but persistence paid off. My review was short and sweet, and read: "And the part of Bill, woodenly played by Al Secunda."

Up until this moment, I had heard people talk about being in emergency situations and having their lives pass before their very eyes, but I always had difficulty relating to this concept. Now I suddenly had an enormous amount of empathy. Everything whizzed past me. Grammar school, high school, college, graduate school, a promising career at William Morris Agency, and now, one million copies of "And the part of Bill, woodenly played by Al Secunda" circulating around Manhattan.

As I stood there in disbelief, the snow increased in intensity, and the bundle of nineteen papers seemed much heavier. Suddenly, the horror of the situation hit me even deeper. In a little more than an hour I was going to have to be up onstage again.

For my own survival purposes, I immediately searched for any salvageable meaning from this review. Well, I thought, at least he didn't say plastic. He did say wood. Wood was at least once alive. Wood was organic, it was nice to look at and feel. Maybe it was even a positive acting term – "the wonderful walnut nature of Brando's work" or "the mahogany running through Hoffman's character." I told you, I was a desperate man. What a perfect time to be kidnapped, I thought.

After destroying all twenty copies of the evidence, I somehow dragged myself down into the subway station and back up to the theater. I prayed that everyone in the cast would be kind and pretend that they hadn't read my review.

As I entered the theater, I did my best not to make eye contact with anyone. I was successful until I made a sharp left turn and literally bumped right into the arms of the director. As our eyes automatically met, I knew that he knew, and he knew that I knew. We kept looking at each other in a long, painful silence. He chose to break the awkwardness by delivering a line that felt more like a bullet through my heart. He opened his arms, tilted his head, and moaned, "My Pinocchio."

Well, if I wasn't suicidal before, I was then. A half hour before show time and my very supportive director gives his "woodenly" leading man badly needed encouragement by calling him Pinocchio. Fearing additional advice and support from Geppetto, I quickly wobbled past him and crawled into my dressing room. After sitting there for a while I somehow pulled myself together and thought more about the review. Well, the good news was that the reviewer at least killed me quickly. He could have dragged it on for pages. I then thought about the reality of my performance. Could I put my ego aside and learn anything from the review? I knew I wasn't "woodenly," but what was I? What I realized was that what the reviewer had seen and called wood was a full-blown case of fear and terror.

I also realized that what was causing a lot of my stage fright was my inauthenticity. In a desire to please the director, I was trying to do things onstage without the necessary emotions to back them up. I was therefore forcing, or pushing, my feelings. The result was poor, uncomfortable, and strained acting. This, in turn, helped to create fear and terror.

What I decided to do instead was to become more integrated and real with my actions and emotions. While I was still going to deliver the correct lines, stand where I was supposed to stand, and sing the songs correctly, I was not going to overact by attempting to push and fake emotions that weren't there. I was determined to act authentically regardless of how terrible my acting might appear.

Miraculously, I got through the entire second show true to my new commitment. Although I didn't have a great time, it certainly was less painful. Afterward, fearing that the director was going to strangle me for changing my entire approach, I attempted to slip out the back of the theater. Unfortunately, he caught me just before I could escape. He grabbed my arm, looked me straight in the eyes, and said, "That was more like it."

More like it? You mean I had to go 180 degrees away from what I thought he wanted, in order to have him say, "That was more like it"? Wow! What a concept. What I learned from my *Barroca* experience was that while we obviously need feedback from others, ultimately, we must get comfortable with our own self-expression. If, by attempting to please others, we are causing pain, struggle, and inauthenticity within ourselves, we must seek out a more truthful, authentic, and nurturing way to perform. Just as the horse must come before the cart, in life comfort and integrity must come before pleasing anyone else.

conclusion

*No pessimist ever discovered the secrets of the stars, or
sailed to an uncharted land, or opened a new heaven
to the human spirit.*

—*Helen Keller*

After my book *Ultimate Tennis* was published, I was invited to
appear on a television show in Japan. After visiting Tokyo and
taping the program, I decided to fly to Hong Kong and visit
my old friend John Holsinger. John was my first great tennis
teacher and was responsible for reigniting my passion for the
sport. During the visit, I told him about a problem I was having
with my forehand stroke. Several months earlier I had begun losing control and confidence in it. Something was wrong and I
couldn't figure out what it was. All I knew was that it kept getting
worse. John agreed to take a look at it.

The next day, John drove me down to the Hong Kong Tennis
Club. We went onto a court, and he hit an entire basket of balls to
my forehand side. Afterward, I ran up to the net and anxiously
awaited his diagnosis. When John arrived, he had a wide smirk on
his face.

"So, did you see what I'm doing wrong?" I asked.

His smirk got even larger. "Yes," he responded.

"So, tell me," I pleaded.

"I'll tell you," he said. "But the answer to your problem lies in
a question."

"Okay, Great Sphinx, let's have the question," I said.

John responded with, "When was the last time you read chapter one of your own book?"

We both began to howl with laughter. Chapter 1 in *Ultimate Tennis* deals with relaxation and fluidity. Apparently, my concern about the forehand had caused me to start using excessive tension in my fingers. This, in turn, caused my entire arm and shoulder to be extremely tense when I was producing my strokes. This excessive tension caused me to lose control and confidence in my forehand.

The point is that it's not enough to know the proper information. What's as important is the application and reapplication of it. Just because we write about a subject, teach it, or preach it, this doesn't mean that we always remember to do it. This is why mastery is an ongoing process. We must always remain humble and inquisitive students in our chosen endeavors. In addition, because we will never arrive at a finite place called "mastery," we must remember occasionally to take time out, to look back, and to celebrate how far we have come.

The 15 Second Principle is really a journey into self-intervention and self-correction. It's about choice, freedom, balance, and well-being. It's about reminding ourselves that while we each have a personal history, we are not our histories. It's about giving up our constant need for control, approval, and results. It's about learning which impulses to act upon and which impulses to ignore. It's about dismantling old conversations, beliefs, and habits in order to build a more viable and vibrant future. It's about embracing more and bracing less. It's about caring less while not being careless. It's about stamina, resiliency, and rejuvenation. It's about giving ourselves permission to succeed and fail. It's about putting at risk what we have become, in order to experience who and what we just might be.

Perhaps the four most challenging aspects of this book are The 15 Second Agreement, the Inclusion Factor, the Pleasure Priority, and the Door Process.

First, staying committed to our 15 Second Agreement will be very difficult. There will be times when we will forget or be afraid to live up to our agreement. Whenever this occurs we must remember to *forgive ourselves*. The sooner we can apply self-forgiveness, the easier it will be to recommit to The 15 Second Principle. In addition, we need to keep remembering that mini-actions produce mini-breakthroughs, which in turn can create major changes in every aspect of our lives.

Second, the Inclusion Factor reminds us to develop a more congenial relationship with the things in ourselves that we hate the most. Because what we resist will persist, it's best to make room for and embrace the things in us that we detest. Also remember that suffering occurs in the struggle, in the resistance, in the straddling of two worlds, not in doing the actual work. As soon as something is integrated and accepted, it will tend to become less of a problem and will begin to dissolve.

Third, the Pleasure Priority encourages us to place pleasure (relaxation, energy, focus, and faith) before precision (goals, targets, and results). Stay patiently devoted to this concept, because it usually takes a long time to trust fully that the pleasure priority mode is the center and source from which all precise actions emanate.

Fourth, the Door Process invites us to seek out the most uncomfortable and ominous areas of our lives, in order to feel the feelings we dare not feel. By intentionally venturing into the belly of the beast, and expanding our capacity to be with these uncomfortable sensations, we will alter our relationship with these off-limit endeavors. This, in turn, will lessen the power and influence that our discomforts and fears have over us.

To assist you in your passionate exploration, I urge you to revisit the material in this book. As your understanding deepens and skills improve, you will glean different insights and messages from the same pages. By slowly rereading these stories and discussions, you will find it less threatening and more exciting to manifest your dreams.

Well, that's it for now, fellow travelers. Keep faithing and having fun as you courageously follow your dreams and face your fears.

> *There is a vitality, a life force, a quickening that is translated through you into action, and because there is only one of you in all time, this expression is unique.*
>
> *And if you block it, it will never exist through any other medium and be lost. The world will not have it. It is not*

your business to determine how good it is: nor how it com-
pares with other expressions. It is your business to keep it
yours clearly and directly to keep the channel open.

You do not even have to believe in yourself or your work.
You have to keep open and aware directly to the urges that
motivate YOU …

—Martha Graham to Agnes DeMille

Al Secunda is a motivational speaker, workshop leader and personal and business consultant. His professional journey has taken him through the fields of business, writing, acting, music, and tennis. He has appeared on many national television shows and has lectured worldwide. Al received his MBA degree in Behavioral Science Management from New York University. He has dedicated his life to the art of mastery and the pursuit of passion, persistence, and productivity. Al resides in Los Angeles, California, and can be visited at www.the15secondprinciple.com.

Self Motivation

Gael Lindenfield

This best-selling title teaches you how to be a success without the fear of failure pulling you back.

Self motivation is an essential skill for success. This practical self-help guide reveals what it is, how exactly it can help us and why it is often so elusive. Presented in a highly readable form, with cartoons and illustrations, the book contains exercises and provides a complete self-help course. Gael Lindenfield – Britain's best known writer on self-esteem and self-confidence – reveals 36 secrets for motivating yourself plus tips on encouraging others to do the same.

So often, low self-esteem can hold us back from achieving our full potential and with the skills Gael offers, the reader will be encouraged to accept challenges, no longer put things off or procrastinate, choose the easy option or indulge in self doubt.

Take Yourself to the Top

Laura Berman-Fortgang

How the Secrets of a Leading Life Coach will Help You Achieve Success

The latest trend in personal development is life coaching: it's somewhere between having a personal trainer and a therapist, someone to check up on you and make sure you are doing what you need to do to achieve your personal and professional goals. Life Coaches focus on the future not the past, they look at obstacles to success and filfilment not to open them up for introspection but to overcome them and achieve goals.

In this excellent, practical guide – Fortgang acts as the reader's own personal life coach. She shares her secrets for getting out of a rut, learning how to go beyond 'just getting by' and taking charge. She also includes many inspiring case studies from her own clients. This book is for those ready to make the leap to the next level of success.

Principles of Stress Management

Vera Peiffer

Principles of Stress Management explains what stress is, how it causes physical and mental problems and how to cope successfully with the increased pressures of modern day living. The book introduces the reader to the stress-prone personality types, what the potential stress triggers are, and suggests effective exercises to help you relax.

Covering the physical stress symptoms and behavioural problems associated with stress – such as compulsive behaviour – the book shows why the scourge of modern day Western living needs to be understood and beaten.

Whether you are a perfectionist, ambitious, anxious, or stimulus-seeking person, the book will be an invaluable eye-opener – a key to learning to deal with stress positively.

Your Best Year Yet

Jinny Ditzler

This book holds the key to making the next 12 months your best ever. Start by answering just 10 key questions and you will have an easy one-page plan for the year ahead. It sounds simple, but by the end of the book you will have turned your most challenging personal issues into a remarkable and powerful practical plan. And it works

'This is the only effective self-help process I know that is transformational, produces focused goals and can actually be completed in 3–4 hours. It gives you the highest, quickest return I have ever seen.'
Dr Charles E. Smith, author of *The Merlin Plan*

'"Best Year Yet" is a positive and powerful concept. Every leader and manager – in fact everyone – could use this approach to help mobilise themselves for achievement.'
Lawrence Churchill, Managing Director, NatWest Life and Investment Services

Thorsons
Directions for life